AF229439

SHAKESPEARE BIOGRAPHY

Shakespeare Biography

And

Other Papers

Chiefly Elizabethan

By

FELIX E. SCHELLING

Essay Index Reprint Series

BOOKS FOR LIBRARIES PRESS
FREEPORT, NEW YORK

First Published 1937
Reprinted 1968

LIBRARY OF CONGRESS CATALOG CARD NUMBER:
68-26473

PRINTED IN THE UNITED STATES OF AMERICA

To my Friends and Fellows

of the

Shakspere Society of Philadelphia

A Prefatory Word

THE papers constituting this volume center in Shakespeare and the Elizabethan age; but they extend into the precincts of my "shop" in "The Study of English," and into personal appraisement and appreciation in the papers commemorating two of the most notable men whom it has been my privilege intimately to know. Horace Howard Furness was essentially an Elizabethan in his charming old-time courtesy and his scholarly and purposeful use of his leisure, living, in his Shakespeare studies from day to day, in that spacious age, as few men of later times have been able to live in it. And Weir Mitchell, grand seigneur that he was in mien and carriage, recurred again and again to that gracious time of inspiration, in his verse, in his conversation, and in his affections. It is not, then, without some basis that I claim for this volume a species of unity in itself, and a congruity with what I have hitherto written. Shall walls of brass bind in the fancy? Or the insidious parallel run only in predestined limits? The bountiful Elizabethan map, with its liberal augmentation of the Indies, excluded neither prophecy nor panegyric.

Contents

CONTENTS

Shakespeare Biography

A SUMMER or two ago, in the seclusion of a French-speaking Swiss town which I love and frequent, I ran across a paper-backed volume entitled *Le Voyage de Shakespeare*. The author is a contemporary Parisian journalist, M. Léon Daudet; save for certain revolutionary-monarchic irregularities of conduct, the undistinguished son of a distinguished father. The copy of this book which I bought is one of the eleventh edition. Evidently they read such books in France; it is even in a way readable. And it tells how Shakespeare, now twenty years of age, "a poet, and therefore subject to dreams and melancholy," sets out from Dover to Rotterdam (wife and babies left behind—presumably another mark of the poet); how he is impelled by a force which "urges him to seek the unknown" (there was nothing unknown in England to Shakespeare at twenty); how he meets with the riot and ribaldry of Dutch burgher life at a period immediately following the assassination of William the Silent, observing, meditating, and moralizing; discussing endlessly politics, religion, philosophy, with publicans and sinners, with reformers and the unregenerate, with anybody, everybody —and, mark you, chiefly in German! For "Shakespeare, thanks to his father, had spoken that tongue from his infancy"! Why, I wonder, should a Frenchman imagine a German-speaking Shakespeare! The first Hebrew he meets suggests Shylock, and his daughter Jessica as well. In a drunken and obese, but companionable, Dutch host —there being none such in England—he finds Falstaff. In a distracted old beggar who imagines himself a king and whom he meets in a storm, we have Lear. Swearing by his Plutarch, which he carries in his bosom and cherishes as a breviary, he wanders aimlessly about. A moonlit night, a fair woman, the lighted windows of a town, transport the impressionable youth, and reduce him either to tears or to the rapid improvisation of "poetry"—in one case an eclogue on drunkenness (*un éloge de l'ivresse*), happily not preserved by our chronicler.

At Delft, Leyden, Amsterdam, amid protracted bouts of theology and drinking, this "Shakespeare" makes his experiencing way, amazed at the commonplace and enchanted with the obvious. In the upshot, true to the traditions of "Gallic life," shall we call it—or is it only Gallic fiction?—he plays a somewhat incredible Adonis to a thawed-out little Danish Venus, and at last, meeting with a troupe of wandering players at Elsinore—where we should rather have expected him to meet with a ghost—he has his genius awakened by means of a frankly sensual intrigue with a fascinating and much experienced actress, who strings him on, a momentary bead on a long necklace of like transient infatuations. Here is a recent Shakespeare! a bit of impressionistic biography for you; if serious enough to be given a name, a piece of the biography of preconception. In such, facts are of a negligible unimportance.

It may well be imagined that M. Daudet would make no serious claim for his production. And nobody about whom it matters in the least is likely to be troubled, much less deceived, by such trifles of an unskilled imagination, or by the unhappy persistency of those strange people who still search variously and hysterically for somebody of at least the rank of a lord as the author of productions so dignified as are these Shakespearean dramas.

Less preposterous, and for that very reason perhaps the more dangerous, are the biographies of purpose, written to prove or disprove something or other which might well have astonished the subject, or to sustain some theory with which the author has become obsessed. A recent example of such a book is a novel about Shakespeare by Clara Longworth, Countess de Chambrun, who is much addicted to this sort of thing; it is rather cleverly conceived as supposedly derived from the recollections of John Lacy, an old Elizabethan actor, and communicated to John Aubrey the anecdotist.[1] It accepts most of the exploded traditions, among them that stubborn Restoration slander of worthy Mistress Davenant as "the dark lady"; but the purpose of the book is to show the poet as existing in the midst of the recusants' perils that beset the religious intrigues and persecutions of the reign, and to prove Shakespeare—as has often been argued—a devotee of the Roman Church. Of course we need not believe, unless we prefer to, that a confession of the older faith alone could have rendered possible these works of dramatic genius; and there are more damaging obsessions and more dangerous theories than such as these. Within a very few years there died a man of brilliant journalistic ability, who wrote a book on the basis of a conviction that the white heat of genius must necessarily sear the soul of man. The journalist was generalizing from his personal and petty experiences, and, mistaking that clever poseur, his friend Oscar Wilde, for an exemplar of genius, found in his despicable criminality and his awful fate an analogue, if not a parallel, for what he determined must have been the misconduct and the fate of Shakespeare. In this book, by the exercise of the reporter's trained sense for scandal and the bias which a search for any definite kind of thing must always entail, he reaches the outrageous conclusion that the price which the world has paid for these highest manifestations of

[1] *Two Loves I Have*, 1934.

drama and poetry, the plays of Shakespeare, was the moral overthrow and wreck of the greatest of human minds. It is deplorable that this was, not long since, the cheapest "Life" of Shakespeare on the American book market; and, for its dragging of a great name in the mire, not the less read.[2]

Biography is a diverse and difficult art; as diverse as are the bare annals of a chronicle and the highly finished products of the fine art of the novelist or the dramatist. And, like all historical writing, biography swings from the gathering, the ordering, and the labeling of what we rejoice to call "facts," to delicate apprehensions of taste, to subtle distinctions in matters of the spirit, and those larger relations to the elements of space and time by means of which we set in order the possessions of the mind. If one is to build a house—the writing of biography is very like such an undertaking—there is, of course, first of all the material. At times it is scanty, at others embarrassingly rich. Whether one or the other, all must be known and considered; and grateful we are to those indefatigable scholars who seek courageously in the dust bins of time for every little trifle that may add to the sum of our knowledge, correct what has been misapprehended, and lead to a truer understanding. For, after all, what is a trifle? Or, at least, who can tell? In Professor Hotson's recent interesting discovery as to Shakespeare, we have, to begin with, a trivial fact, to wit, that Shakespeare was bound over with an associate in theatrical ventures, one Francis Langley, not unknown to dramatic annals, to keep the peace as to a certain complainant.[3] Leaving it there, we have nothing of any apparent importance. But who exactly was Langley, and who was the complainant? A quarrel

[2] Frank Harris, *The Man Shakespeare and his Tragic Life-Story*, 1909.
[3] *Shakespeare versus Shallow*, 1931.

usually precedes such a binding over to keep the peace. What was it that led up to this quarrel? what were its consequences? and a score of such queries, each offering a lead; questions which can be put and intelligently followed out to a logical issue only by a scholar of Professor Hotson's trained competency—and deeply worthy of consideration become the results. Professor Hotson finds in these, his results, the probable locality of Shakespeare's residence at nearly the height of his activity; his association through Francis Langley with a theatre, the Swan, with which we have not hitherto associated him; a quarrel of these two with a notoriously corrupt local justice of the peace, one William Gardiner, and his stepson and dupe, the variety of human creature that Shakespeare calls a "natural." The interesting inference that associates these two opponents of the poet with the characters Justice Shallow and Simple, which is perhaps not wholly made out to our satisfaction, and the reference of two, if not three, important plays—*Henry IV* and *The Merry Wives of Windsor*—to dates decidedly earlier than those usually accepted, with the very occasion of the first performance of the latter pointed out on arguable grounds—these are some of the products derivable from this seemingly trifling matter, the suggestion of which and the manner of it are a credit to biographical scholarship.

I have just said that to the proper equipment of the biographer a complete acquaintance with all of the material concerning his subject is a *sine qua non*. And as to any subject in these days of the multiplicity of books, this is asking much. Wherefore our admiration goes out unreservedly to such a scholar as Sir Edmund Chambers, in recognition of his stupendous work in gathering together and ordering the vast material which forms the basis not only of the biography of Shakespeare himself, but of that of his many fellows, together with the data necessary to a reconstruction of the background of it all, constituting a history of the stage and the drama of his time. And yet, precious as are these admirable volumes, and beyond praise for their order, arrangement, and the accessibility of the multiplicity of detail that they contain, is it altogether captious to suggest, returning to our figure, that we have here, after all, merely the material, the piled-up, sorted, and carefully labeled stuff out of which to construct a veritable biography of Shakespeare and a history of the drama of his time? This difference is readily discernible by a comparison of these later works of Sir Edmund with his earlier, wholly admirable book on medieval drama, in which not only is the material presented and appraised, but the whole is rationalized into the continuity of an historical narrative that reads like the work of art that it is.

The discovery of fact, the classification and labeling of material, however admirably accomplished, is not biography. The dates by which we set such store—birth, death, marriage, publication, even those happy illustrative anecdotes that, like straws, indicate just what straws may indicate and no more—all of these are only the material with which to construct such biographical edifices as this, that, or the other architect-in-lives may be at the pains to erect. There are those who are content to pull out a board or two from the pile of lumber and discuss minutely its dimensions; there are those who merely criticize the piling of the lumber; and those who, like the late Frank Harris, unearth something unclean or rotting which they affect to have found under a seemingly decorous exterior. This last is biography with a thesis to sustain, not biography to realize the subject to our understanding. The biographer with a thesis is likely to feel that Shakespeare, the man or his work, is in need of interpretation, historical or esoteric, which he, the biographer, alone can give, and he makes out the dramatist a mere journalist, allegorically and allusively risking his head in treasonable parallels, or he interprets Shakespeare as a transcendent philosopher armed with a prophetic grasp of Hegelianism and all the "isms" that have branched out of it, a species of mouthpiece speaking forth, like an oracle, things beyond his comprehension, to be grasped and elucidated only after three hundred and fifty years by a genius, the commentator, obviously greater than he whom he so interprets to an ignorant world.

That I am not setting up straw men for the pleasure of bowling them over, witness such works as those of a certain Miss Winstanley, who in one entitled *Hamlet and the Scottish Succession* contends, for example, that that great play is merely an allegory of political events involving James, a scholarly prince of thirty, who is Hamlet, and of whom the English really knew little except that he was the likely successor to their throne; involving Mary of Scotland, who is Gertrude, his mother, one who had married Bothwell-Claudius, the murderer of her kingly husband, Darnley—*alias* the elder Hamlet. Miss Winstanley even finds a parallel between the curious mode of this last monarch's death, by poison poured into his ear, and the actual manner in which one of the relations of Mary's first husband, Francis of France, came to his death. Mr. G. Wilson Knight is the esoteric interpreter of Shakespeare in several books, such as *Myth and Miracle, an Essay on the Mystic Symbolism of Shakespeare* (1929) and *The Wheel of Fire* (1930), which interpret for the uninitiated "Shakespeare's sombre tragedies," as he calls them, with a brilliancy and conviction quite transcendental to the normal comprehension. Nor are these alone in their aberrations from the highways of biography.

"Not to interpret, nor disclose, still less to discode, or decypher; but to realize the subject to our understanding": after all, is not this much the function of the biographer, that he shall make his subject so live that we may come to know him as we might come to know someone whom we have met, with whom we have become more or less intimately acquainted; even more, one whom we have had extraordinary opportunities to know, the more especially in those things which have marked him out above other men? The happiest crown to a life of distinction is an understanding biographer. Even the great Dr. Johnson would live less illustriously for us but for his incomparable Boswell. And with the mention of Boswell, the arch-biographer, we have modulated naturally from our material piled high and orderly to the architect himself, the artist-in-lives.

In every biography there is what the chemists call a by-product: it is often almost as important as the product itself. And in biography that by-product manifests itself, often only too unconsciously, in a display of the characteristics, the personality, the prejudices of the biographer. Let us take some of the earliest Shakespearean biographers and critics. Nobody now remembers one William Winstanley, who published his *Lives of the Most Famous English Poets,* in 1686, when the fourth folio of Shakespeare was new on the stalls. But when this biographer tells us of Shakespeare: "By keeping company with Learned persons, and conversing with jocular Wits, whereto he was naturally inclin'd, he became so famously witty, or wittily famous, that by his own industry, without the help of Learning, he attained to an extraordinary height in all strains of Dramatick Poetry," we know that Winstanley was a condescending Oxford don, and a coxcomb. To read Nicholas Rowe's *Some Account of the Life of Mr. Shakespeare,* prefixed to the first eighteenth-century attempt to edit the dramatist's works, is to learn to know a kindly, liberal-hearted gentleman, amateur though he is according to the rigorous standards of complaisant modern scholarship. We feel as to "Mr. Pope, the foremost poet of Europe," that it was a considerable condescension on his part when he undertook to edit the works of a common player of a ruder age, to add judiciously to Shakespeare's beauties with little black splotches of criticism like the moons and stars with which contemporary court ladies heightened their complexions. Whilst to read Dr. Johnson's Preface to his *Shakespeare* is to attend humbly a magisterial court, in which respect for learning and common sense mingles with a feeling of awe for the size of the judge's wig and the thunder of his voice. We feel that Shakespeare is being tried at the bar—and hope that he may be acquitted; for such a judge in a hanging mood would be a terror to behold. There are contemporary books into which this by-product, the personality of the biographer as a critic, obtrudes. Recognizing the abiding rottenness of things in Denmark, unlike Hamlet such a biographer finds it no cursed spite that he was born to set things right. With the historical beagles sniffing out deep political allusion in what we had innocently believed to be harmless comedy, and the high priests declaring to our inferior understandings the inner meanings of "the sombre tragedies"; with one of the critics telling us just what Shakespeare wrote and what he did not write, and another doubting if he really could write at all, we are driven to the extremity of holding all books about Shakespeare in suspicion and to declaring, "I want no interpreter betwixt me and the puppets."

I have been employing the term biography, I am aware, with perhaps an indefensible looseness, to denote not only the formal written life of a man, but any image or reconstruction of him and of what made him the man and the force which he was, from a portrait by pen or pencil, to the idea or ideal which each of us holds in his mind of the personality, the entity that he was. I have never been able to rid myself of the conviction that what we are really after in seeking to know the life of any man is the discovery, or at least an approximation to the understanding, of the essentials in which he rose above other men, not the trivialities in which he showed characteristics common to the mass of mankind. Is it altogether relevant to our knowledge of the novelist called Walter Scott or the poet named Byron to learn that each was lame? (Unless one desires to push the inquiry as to the latter to the point of ascertaining, as someone once suggested, if one of his Lordship's feet was not perhaps actually cloven?) And is it not almost a pity that our search for the only celibate poet in the range of English literature must now halt not even at the young Wordsworth? The literacy, or was it illiteracy, of Shakespeare's father or daughter, the exact degree of the relationship of Shakespeare's mother to the Ardens and back to King Alfred, the absence or the degree of the poet's Latinity, the derivations of his name, and the incredible number of variations in the orthography of it—these are topics to war over and endlessly to discuss. Just where he lived in London; the dangerous vicissitudes conceivable at Oxford from the dark eyes of a slandered Mistress Davenant; how he died—was it of too much revelry with

Ben Jonson or because of the unhygienic conditions of Stratford?—Had he the palsy when he signed his will and why, oh why—let it be said in anguish—did he leave his wife his second-best bed as an after-thought in an interpolated passage of his will? Here are some of the topics that fill the pages of Halliwell-Phillipps, admirable delver into the dust-heaps of the past that he was; such small deer disport in the biographical underbrush and fall prey, the quarry of informative arch-biographers such as the late Sir Sidney Lee. And yet in any portrait, what to omit is almost if not quite as difficult as what to include. We are thrust back again on our architect-in-lives; for the only difference between a notable artist in portraiture and you or me lies in the simple and obvious fact that he knew where to put the strokes; you and I do not. The material is there, the subject is there; it is the sense of design, the knowledge, the skill, the humble sinking of self in the subject, that alone can produce the portraiture, the veritable life that we are seeking.

Biography indeed is not unlike theology, constructive as each must be, in the main, of the unknowable. There is a theology that mythologizes, sometimes very beautifully as did the Greek; and there is a theology that takes us deeply into the consideration of sin and evil, that delights to play at loggats with the bones of long-forgotten scandal, and reduce to a mediocrity of morals, at least, the men of genius who tower intellectually above us. For whether you are an avowed theologian in your biographical processes or a mere layman, we are all of us myth-makers, fashioning often strange gods out of stranger materials, adding our little contributions of worship, of explanation, of invention and distortion; posing as the clever detective, the regenerator who will set things right, the know-all who carries a solution of every mystery in his waistcoat pocket, and—not wholly to be forgotten in his unvocal honesty—the devout and understanding worshiper of heroes.

I confess to a deep-seated preference for that architect-in-lives who makes out of his edifice, circumstances permitting, something in the nature of a place of worship. And by this I do not in the least mean to limit biography to eulogy or to those sugared nothings dressed with opportune obliviousness which we serve only after death. I have in mind as to this phase of biography such an engaging book as that which Fulke Greville wrote and called *The Life of Sir Philip Sidney*. There, in a wilderness of delightful irrelevance, there stand out two objects of the author's devotion: Sir Philip, his boyhood's friend, and their incomparable queen, Elizabeth, both, let us confess, perhaps dilated here to heroic stature, yet both essentially true to those lines of portraiture that are significant as opposed to the trivialities which, emphasized, distort and misrepresent. For example, take this much-quoted passage of Greville as to Sidney: "This was it which, I profess, I loved dearly in him, and still shall be glad to honour in the great men of this time: I mean, that his heart and tongue went both one way, and so with every one that went with the Truth; as knowing no other kindred, partie, or end." Here is an essential feature in Greville's portrait of Sidney, perhaps the essential feature, emphasized with lingering words; and that Sidney was the idol of his time becomes a matter accountable. You may abuse the memory of Queen Elizabeth and accumulate all the petty evidences as to her vanity, her parsimony, her Machiavellian turns and evasions and the like. Having done so to the content of scandal, think of Greville, now an aging and honored counselor of King James, recalling in his study the long-gone days when he and Sidney had run a tilt before their queen, and describing now himself as one "who hath ever since been dying to all those glories of Life which he formerly enjoyed, under the blessed, and blessing presence of this unmatchable Queen and woman." A sovereign who could inspire such loyalty in such a man is proof against the malignity of time; for here is an essential feature in the portrait of a great queen, and a great woman.

Considering the difficulties that beset historical writing, I am almost persuaded that the contemporary, he who has known the man personally and lived with him, is your only true biographer. Such was the admirable Boswell. For where again shall we find that nice balance between adoration and criticism, that delicate confusion of the keenness of observation with the obtuseness of the affections? I fear that if we must have a contemporary for our ideal biographer, we shall be forced over into the neighboring realm of autobiography. There at least we have a certain inevitable kind of truth that will out despite the subterfuges of egotism. Benvenuto Cellini could not conceal in his celebrated autobiography of a great artist, the autobiography of a ruffian and a braggart; nor could Lord Herbert of Cherbury, in his "self-portrait"—horrible word!—of a model gentleman and philosopher, hide the coxcomb and the poseur. Only too well do we know that the contemporary biographer may write his story with a bias; although the deliberate writing up of the life of a man with the purpose of convicting him of as much breakage in the china shop of the ten commandments as possible, appears to be almost a contemporary invention.

And here let us leave biography with all its confidences and reticences. I had once thought that I too at the latter end of a long life of studentship might dare to try my hand at a full-length portrait of the greatest personality that I have ever known, for I have dabbled many a sketch of that great figure in my time and in sundry postures. But it will not do, for I should be proclaimed an idolator, and idolatry is out of date in these our days. Besides there are two other excellent reasons. Why could I dare to hope for success where so many have failed? And lastly, why should I lose the proud distinction which is mine as the only English or American scholar dealing with the Elizabethan age and reaching, shall we say, the age of literary discretion, who has not perpetrated a full length *Life of William Shakespeare?*

A Negative of Shakespeare

When I am in trouble to find out what a thing actually is, I find it often very helpful to ascertain quite definitely what that thing is not. So many positive assertions are made as to Shakespeare, that suppose we attempt, at least as a method of approach, a negative picture, so to speak, and proceed thereafter as does the photographer, by means of this negative to our approximate answer to the question, What is the significance, the meaning, the import of Shakespeare?

One of the things which we are most accustomed to accept is the universality of the Shakespearean mind: and of course the extraordinary range and diversity of his art is not for a moment to be denied. But Shakespeare is not really universally minded; for there are wide provinces in the intellectual, the poetical, even in the dramatic art of his time to which he remained, with all his scope and versatility, a total stranger. There was first of all the religious, the theological world of men like Richard Hooker, celebrated historian of the polity of the Church of England, or the eloquent and deeply learned Dr. Donne, Dean of St. Paul's. The theological province in the sixteenth century was a vast and much debated one. This was the age of the several translations of our English Bible crowned with the version of King James, in print five years before the death of Shakespeare. This was the age of religious controversy and the theological disputation in which universal religious intolerance might declare one a heretic at Rome or a heretic at Geneva. This busy, acrimonious, erudite, and uncharitable world is simply unknown to Shakespeare. Shakespeare never sees things in the theological way.

Secondly, there is the world of scholarship, the domain of books, by which we of the academic world set great store. That world was occupied in Shakespeare's own art of the drama with great distinction by his friend and junior by some ten years, Ben Jonson. Jonson was a learned scholar, and, in his view of mankind, at all times a moralist. He saw life either satirically as a moralist commonly does, or else refracted through books, those spectacles through which scholarship habitually sees things. Now, again, the scholarly, the academic way of looking at things is never Shakespeare's. And he seldom sees things long in a satirical light. It flickers with him occasionally, as in Jaques or Malvolio for example; satire is Jonson's chief illumination.

Once more, in sheer poetry this time; it was Edmund Spenser who inherited the wealth of the middle ages, and a chief article in that wealth was imaginative allegory, the creation of an ideal world to run somewhat parallel, or rather what we think is parallel, to this world of ours, beautiful, fantastic, visionary, but sustained by a high ideality and a moral and philosophical fervor. With respect to this kind of poetic world, it may be confidently affirmed that Shakespeare never sees things in the allegorical way; he is never visionary and he never weights his plays with the leaden clogs of purpose ethical or philosophical, though abundantly both where such belongs to his art. Still again, as to limitations in this kind, Shakespeare is emphatically never scientific or speculative, for each is the antithesis of poetry. You cannot at once analyze a flower botanically, or even theorize as to its place in the scale of living things, and at the same time make it your subject for a picture or a flight of poetry. You can do one thing or the other; the same man rarely, if ever, views nature in both ways. The scientific and speculative field of the age of Elizabeth was regally filled by that intellectual giant in the realms of thought, Francis Bacon; and the wide, if at times somewhat arid fields of his investigations into nature, human speculation, and worldly human conduct, are once more provinces unknown and absolutely alien to the nature, the mind, the heart of the dramatist, the poet Shakespeare. The type of mind which we derive from a study of the philosophical, the scientific, the speculative works which are Bacon's is in every conceivable respect the antithesis, the negation, the denial, of the type of mind which is disclosed in the plays of Shakespeare—a simple truth, the recognition of which might have spared us one of the silliest vagaries of our time. We may summarize up to this point, that Shakespeare is neither theological, academic, satirical, nor allegorical; he is neither skeptical and inquisitive after the manner of the scientific man, nor is he speculative after the manner of the metaphysician or the philosopher. Here are already seven huge provinces in human intellectual activity in which Shakespeare is not only not a prince, but in which he scarcely owns an acre.

To descend to lesser, but still significant, things: Shakespeare is not rationalistic and atheistical in his ideas, as was alleged of Marlowe. Shakespeare was not blatantly egotistical like John Marston, another fellow dramatist, who had the impertinence to dedicate his works to oblivion, as though such a precaution were ever necessary. Shakespeare was not a rhetorician, daintily picking out pretty expressions and "running the letter," like Lyly the Euphuist; he never affects a difficult diction, as did Browning in our own late time; nor does he wrap up his wisdom in cabalistic obscurity, like his fellow-poet Chapman, the famous translator of Homer. Especially be it remembered that Shakespeare was never convicted, self-confessed, of bribery and corruption in office like a certain great lord and chancellor of England, infinitely above him in worldly station, named Francis Bacon. Nor did Shakespeare ever kill a man, like Ben Jonson, who killed two; nor was he killed in a disreputable broil in a tavern like poor Marlowe; nor did he die of a surfeit of "pickled herring and Rhenish," the ridiculous end of the bad life of Robert Greene. Why, Shakespeare, quite unlike nearly every one of his fellow dramatists, does not even so much as mention tobacco, though he believed, in his own confession, in both "cakes and ale"; Shakespeare's petty limitations, like his great ones, are many and startling. It is quite amazing how many things Shakespeare did not do, did not say, or bother his head about. Here we have fifteen exclusions, some of them of considerable moment, of regions unknown or untraversed by him, of things that he could not do or that he would not.

Even in his own art, that royal domain of his, the subject of which, I take it, from beginning to end is man, humanity, our own kind in all our human variety and complexity—even in his own domain there are definite limitations. Shakespeare is not interested in man as a scientific investigator is obviously interested in him. He does not wish to know man physically or biologically. Nor does he seek to class him anthropologically. I am almost disposed to deny that Shakespeare is interested in man psychologically, at least as we have come to think of that desperate, shifting, impertinently prying science, if science it always contrives to remain. Yet the quest of the dramatist in Shakespeare's age seems to have been no narrow one, comprising, as it did, an effort to know mankind from below, where we border upon the beasts, to our hopes, our ambitions and aspirations, in which some of us, however few the number, may claim a kinship with the angels. It would seem to me that such a quest into humanity as this might well be put alongside of Bacon's famous boast about taking all learning for his province; though Shakespeare appears not to

power to cure by touch is lugged in, to say nothing of the witches, a favorite royal topic, we must exclude Shakespeare from the list of flatterers of royalty. Almost as absurd is the idea that the dramatist hated common people. Shakespeare does not like mobs; and he represents them humorously and good-naturedly, knowing that they are fickle and dangerous. But he is fair to the common man, however he does find fools in his class as in all classes. The limitations of Shakespeare in the historical plays were not an under-sympathy with mobs and an over-sympathy with kings; his limitations here lie in the unwieldiness of his material and in national prejudice. I hate to think of the representation of Joan of Arc in *Henry VI;* a consoling opinion is that it is not really Shakespeare's work. It is a gorgeous pageant, this of Shakespeare's historical dramas, gracious, breathing, tragic, pathetic, realizing hundreds of personages and scores of events with a vividness and an insight rare in any form of historical composition. And all this is because, playing the game of a chronicle of historical events presented on a limited stage with inadequate personnel and equipment equally inadequate to represent anything at all like actual historical event, Shakespeare triumphed over these lets and hindrances, as far as success could lie within these self-accepted limitations.

In the comedies we come nearer to the dramatist's own everyday life, and in them better than elsewhere we find how contemporaneous Shakespeare is: still another limitation, if you like. The men and women of these plays are essentially English men and English women; more narrowly still, they are Elizabethan men and Elizabethan women. There is nothing to show that Shakespeare ever traveled abroad; though travel abroad does not seem to be, even in our day, particularly destructive of provincialism and insularity.

Some of Shakespeare's Welshmen, Frenchmen, Irish and the like display this last quality in their creator. Even Shakespeare shared our human mistrust of that which we do not know any too well. It is the dramatist's frank, almost childlike, translation of the wealth of the story of the world into the familiar terms of his own age that is one of the sources of his power. A great observer, a man possessed of what Bagehot calls the "experiencing nature," can know his own world with an intimacy and exactness, an understanding, which could never be that of even the profoundest scholar who is trying to reconstruct the historical past, or even the foreign present. I repeat that Shakespeare's characters are essentially Elizabethan in speech, manners, conduct, mode of thinking, even in costume. The doublet and hose covered them all; and Juliet, Portia, Rosalind, all are English girls, as their lovers, fathers, husbands, and friends are English men, however exotic the names given them and their designated habitations. But what an age to be translated into, even with all its limitations remembered! An age of old-time courtesy in manners, of respect for years and station, of dutiful and faithful service; one in which there was still leisure, and much that could not be bought; in which articles of daily use were wrought by artisans, not manufactured in factories, and neither conduct, dress, speech, nor spelling was standardized. Spenser's *Faerie Queene* is poetry transcendent, an imaginative ideal beyond the time, unreal, now out of date in its vestments if not in its aspiration. Such is true of much of the lesser poetry of the old age, and of more of the contemporary lesser drama. But the greater plays of Shakespeare, be they tragedy or comedy, constitute a drama of such a verity to human nature, that, imaginative and poetical as they are, they remain, in the large, of a universal applicability and are as contemporary today as they were when

Shakespeare wrote them. Shakespeare did not transcend his age, he realized it; and in realizing the essentials, the things that last, of his own age, he realized the features common to all times, the traits that make men men.

In the tragedies, Shakespeare's draughts on experience in life become deeper, and we find him sounding the depths of human suffering and human crime in a process none the less based on that intimate knowledge that comes to one who has been born with the gift of intuition, with a sympathy for others in which egotism is forgotten, and a charity in judgment of the conduct of others which is as precious as it is unparalleled. In history Shakespeare was trammeled with the past, even if he does interrupt the conspirators in *Julius Caesar* with the striking of a clock and invite Cleopatra to a game of billiards. In comedy the limitations of his art were its contemporaneousness, those little touches and intimate allusions—to the sports, the handicrafts, the current happenings and slang of the moment—things that brought the play home to the bosoms of his hearers, but matters that we, his posterity, have to dig out learnedly by means of notes. In the tragedies the dramatist is nearer to naked humanity, for all these accidents of custom, manners, speech, and allusion to things current are as garments in contrast to those primal passions of love, jealousy, greed, ambition, pride and the like, which are the common birthright of man and little affected by his accidental surroundings. This is why, after all, Shakespeare comes nearer to us in the great tragedies than elsewhere. This is why Hamlet, Macbeth, Lear, Antony, and Othello remain in our minds with Ophelia, Lady Macbeth, Cordelia, Cleopatra, and Desdemona, as actual contemporary people, alive and vivid as they have been and will be, realities and a topic for deep pondering in each generation, not even to be hurt very much by dressing them up in our own passing ridiculous costume and confusing their actions with our own trivial conventionalities.

But even in his own day Shakespeare was subject to limitations which we sometimes fail to remember. Aside from the fact that even he is not always at his best, that there are times when, like Homer, he nods, and many more in which he must have felt that he failed of his own ideals, there were his auditors and what they demanded. For I agree, and heartily, with the contention of the critics that a play is a something to be acted, that in its completeness we have in happy conjunction the playwright, the actors, the scene, the action, dialogue, light, costume, ensemble, and that most incalculable quantity in the equation, the audience. Shakespeare was affected by his audience and undoubtedly strove to give it what it wanted. It is a tribute to that audience that it appreciated such plays. And it is the last error that we should fall into, to belittle the men whose approval, backed by their money, made Shakespeare. The Elizabethan audience was a representative one from courtier and lord, patrons of the arts who sat on the stage, to the groundlings, common fellows, tapsters and apprentices, who stood in the yard. Such an auditory was at least as quick of response as ours, less sophisticated, more widely acquainted with the theatre and acting than we, if happily less read. It must have been an inspiration to write for such, if somewhat less so for the more cultivated, critical, and knowing audience of the Court. Shakespeare was limited in his day by the simplicity, the crudeness of his stage, although even these limitations had advantages. For example, the old stage, extending into the middle of the room with the auditors close about it, afforded an opportunity beyond our usual one, for a display of the niceties of declamation, action, and facial expression. The comparative absence —for it was but comparative—of what we designate as scenery, also contributed further to center the interest in the actor; and the very simplicity of the accessories stimulated thought and attention in the auditor to make himself a veritable party to the understanding and enjoyment of the play.

These were some of Shakespeare's advantages. The disadvantages are more apparent to us than they were to him. Our American forefathers traveled in delight in stage coaches and canal boats and, a little anxious about the excessive speed of the former, suffered no prophetic nightmares as to railroads, automobiles, and flights into space. The lights of the Elizabethan stage—when they used them—were candles; the costumes were contemporary. As late as Garrick, Macbeth was acted in the uniform of a British major general and Cleopatra in prodigious hoop-skirts once called farthingales: Antony could never have arrived within a furlong of such a Cleopatra. But then, the happy Elizabethans, except perhaps for Ben Jonson, scarcely gave the matter of costume a thought. A king wears a crown, and a Roman a sort of cloak called a toga; a rich man wears fine clothes and a beggar rags; a crook for a shepherd and a gown for a scholar, and they let it go at that. Once more, it is hard to keep remembering that Shakespeare never saw a woman on the stage; we escape from that sight so rarely. He may have heard that there were actresses in Italy and France, and being no Puritan, he was probably not greatly shocked. But this thing was against the English tradition. Wherefore it cannot but give us pause to think of the marvelous succession of Shakespeare's women, so true to womanhood, at times so lovely, so genuinely refined and womanly, and all of them, from Juliet to Imogen, loveliest of them all, acted by little boys whose voices had not yet changed into manhood. Do you recall the pretty badinage of the epilogue of *As You Like It,* the point of which is wholly lost unless you remember that the boy, pretending to be Rosalind, and the Rosalind, pretending to be a boy, is really a boy and not an actress; and Cleopatra's famous horror lest in the coming triumph of Augustus,

> the quick comedians
> Extemporally will stage us and present
> Our Alexandrian revels; . . .
> and I shall see
> Some squeaking Cleopatra boy my greatness
> I' the posture of a whore,[1]

is a notable example of Shakespeare's consciousness of the nature of this limitation. And is it wholly a limitation? Without falling into a diatribe as to that ubiquitous appeal to sex on our contemporary stage that makes it difficult for an old Victorian, such as the author, to read the play awarded a prize a year ago, without an unpleasurable sense of complicity in impropriety, there is something to say for a recent opinion of Mr. Granville Barker who remarks of Shakespeare: "His studies of women seem often to be begun from some spiritual paces beyond the point at which a modern dramatist leaves off. . . . Curious that not a little of the praise lavished upon the beauty and truth of them—mainly by women—may be due to their having been written to be played by boys." [2]

I might dwell on still other limitations, conspicuous among them the fact that the playwright wrote for a definite group of actors

[1] *Antony and Cleopatra,* V, ii, 206–219.

[2] *Prefaces to Shakespeare,* First Series, 1933, p. xxix.

whose limitations as well as their capabilities entered into his problem, as the many definite allusions in these plays make certain: a Juliet fourteen years of age, a Hamlet "fat and scant of breath," the lankiness of Andrew Aguecheek, the girth of Falstaff. But we have enough.[3]

There is little need for recapitulation. Shakespeare presents, like any other highly specialized being, human or other, an extraordinary list of limitations; for I give no acceptance to Carlyle's primitive conception of a universal heroical stuff out of which pretty much any kind of hero can be made. It is a familiar saying of men of adventurous life that one can scarcely be expected at once to live an epic and to write one; and perhaps the reverse is equally true. That Shakespeare's outward life was peculiarly uneventful is not to be denied. He sailed not around the world with Francis Drake nor trafficked in slaves with Hawkins. He died not of wounds in chivalrous fight as did Sidney, nor on the scaffold, a constructive traitor, like Raleigh. Even an autobiographical interpretation of the *Sonnets* presents, alas, no surprising or unhuman story, except for the fact that those who are subdued by vice, as some of our modern scandalmongers would have us believe that Shakespeare was subdued, do not see with the ethical vision of this sonneteer. But if the outward life of this most human of men was uneventful, what an adventure into the realms of art must it have been to have arrived at the artistic realization of a Hamlet, a Macbeth, an Othello! What adventures of the spirit must have been those of the creator,—I prefer to say "realizer,"—of these scores on scores of personages that laugh and love and live through these consummate dramas!

[3] See especially the suggestive chapter on "Actors in Shakespeare's Plays" in T. W. Baldwin, *The Organization and Personnel of the Shakespearean Company,* 1927.

Let it be repeated that Shakespeare was not a bookish man: he saw life direct, not distorted into satire and criticism nor skeptically doubted and questioned; least of all did he see through any other man's spectacles. Wherefore when he wrote, he took the material nearest to his hand in a chronicle, an Italian story or an English one, better still and more usually, an earlier English play—and he fashioned it and shaped it, turning often a shapeless lump into a product of artistic beauty and meaning. In this artistic process of his, Shakespeare, busy with something else, was little troubled with much of the luggage that we feel very necessary for even a short journey into the land of fiction. He was bothered, for example, not at all with doctrines and schemes for the salvation of man's soul in another world, but accepted as part of this world its various forms of religious faith, even its petty obsessions and superstitions. It was not his business to rationalize and speculate, much less to unmask accepted beliefs. Shakespeare appears to have wasted little time in ridiculing the superstitions of other people. This trait of his has worried some rigorous souls who insistently want to know exactly how everybody stands and has always stood about everything, who yearn to settle him on their own solid footing rather than on his own. By the same token, Shakespeare left politics to such as care for that particular human game, recognizing the political passion as one incident to man, and to form therefore a part of his picture. What Shakespeare's personal opinions about government may have been it is not so difficult to infer. He seems to have recognized "degree" as he calls it, or station in life, which hardly appears to me much more than an acceptance of the world as it is. His company was involved in some difficulty because, at the time of the Essex conspiracy, his *Richard II,* in which that king was dethroned, was acted "to hearten the conspirators," amongst whom was Shakespeare's early patron, the Earl of Southampton. On James's accession Shakespeare's company became the King's, by a clever business coup, not a political one. Shakespeare even set some store, it would appear, by the coat of arms of the Shakespeares, for which he endeavored to procure a grant by the college of heralds. Let the man who does not care a hang for the respectability of his own family cast the first stone.

As to his own art of the stage, the great dramatist was far too interested in writing his two plays a year to theorize about how to do it, though the age was full, as has ever been ours, of patter about "the precepts of Aristotle" and other learned discussions of technique. Moreover, Shakespeare was far too immersed in the personages of his creation to be in the least concerned with that obsession of small minds, the expression of one's self. And he appears to have interested himself little in the matter of originality. If you happen to be born an authentic creative sovereign,—as was Shakespeare, if ever there has been a king,—you may take your own by divine right, wherever you find it. And therefore the supreme dramatist rarely bothers himself to invent a story or even an incident. And the marvel is how efficiently and completely he makes everything he takes his own, stamping upon it the sign manual of his royalty. Need we wonder then that "the grand style" is Shakespeare's in these plays where the passion and the dignity of the subject demand it? "The grand style" was just as much a part of the life of that stately age as were its satins and brocades, its embroidered stomachers, its furred gowns, its ruffs and falling bands. At the other extreme where it belongs, what slang is racier or more smacking of the moment than that of Falstaff and his rout? Shakespeare knew that

Cleopatra herself could have presented no more infinite variety than does human nature, of which even Egypt's queen with all her fascinations was but a single example. He knew that beauty is in life, and ugliness, heroism and sin, devotion and selfishness, and he was no more afraid of any one of these than of any other. Among the many qualities of this, our superlative dramatist, I place his courage almost highest. Artistically, he was afraid of nothing; he could, on occasion, stake all and win. He could conceive of a beauty and an ideality in human conduct above your imagining or mine; and he could find it in his heart to extend his charity and his understanding to personages with whom you or I might hesitate to associate.

The significance of Shakespeare lies, it would seem to me, especially in two great qualities of his art, based deeply in the fundamental qualities of his great nature. And the first of these is his unaffected fidelity to the realities, the actualities of human life, which he never shirks, extenuates, or tampers with in his art. This first great quality of the Shakespearean art is sustained on a matchless observation and a true rendering of things seen, heard, and experienced, a rendering that seldom flags, and is, again and again, exceedingly daring. The second great quality of Shakespeare is his equal faithfulness to the ideality and the aspirations of our human life, sustained as it is by a vision, an imagination, an airy litheness and agility of mind beyond these qualities in all other poets. When the poet informs the dramatist, and the dramatist informs the poet, we reach the highest expression of that art which is devoted to the delineation of human feeling and human conduct by means of the spoken word. Still once more, forming the basis of both those artistic qualities in supreme craft, we have the solid ethical foundation which shows us Shakespeare the most law-abiding yet withal the bravest, the most liberal moralist among the sons of man. Whatever may or may not be true of the peccadilloes of the human life that was his—and let us not believe scandal of any man, leastways of the great—here is an artist who exhibits in the code of his art that fine double standard of morals whereby not the laws of Mede or Persian shall more strictly rule than I shall rule myself and my personal conduct, but to my fellow men let me extend all the understanding, the sympathy, the extenuation that thought can devise, and a forgiveness that wipes out all recollection of sometime sin or failure. It is a precious possession, this high Shakespearean ideal, in an uncharitable world, for above his drama, which is truth, and his poetry, which is beauty, is this attitude of mind which chimes with the words of a greater even than Shakespeare, "And the greatest of these is charity."

The significance of Shakespeare is manifold, and this significance lies almost as much, as we have seen, in what Shakespeare was not as in what he was. I believe Shakespeare to have been a man of fine presence and good voice, or his fellow actors would never have entrusted to him the dignified part of the ghost of buried Denmark which tradition relates that he acted in *Hamlet*.[4] I believe that Shakespeare was a man of dutiful conduct, alike from the circumstance that he was honest in his theatrical trade and paid his taxes, and because he provided for his family and returned home as soon as he was able to live among those who had always known him. I believe Shakespeare to have been a man of sound judgment, for he prospered in his trade; of warm friendships which he sought little among those socially above him, but among his fellow players and playwrights. And I find in his plays an abundant cheerfulness, de-

[4] Recorded earliest apparently by Rowe, *Works of Shakespeare*, 1709, p. vi.

spite some rainy days, a kindliness of attitude towards all mankind and, let me repeat, a universal charity. His consummate drama apart, his transcendent poetry aside, this man of the largest human heart moved equally at home in the midst of the ostentation of royalty or among the bacchanalian revels of the Boar's-Head Tavern; conversant with wisdom and bandying jocularity with the fool, he descended below human kind in fish-like brutish Caliban, foreshadowing "the missing link" of the biologists, and he transcended equally mankind in the spirit Ariel, who enters "invisible" in one scene of *The Tempest* to breathe across, a gentle zephyr, in another. This man of largest heart hated scarcely one of his kind and, among the beautiful things that he loved was music and, his own word for it—for this, too, is music—"a low voice in woman."

Veritably the greatest miracle of it all lies in this: that the wisest, the kindliest, most charitable and understanding mind that the world has yet produced should have been, not some mighty prelate, an archbishop at least, with the theological learning of the centuries at his beck and call; not some memorable philosopher, dwelling aloof in contemplation of remote stars; not even a wise prince, such as Marcus Aurelius, living, safe in his own integrity, in the midst of a wicked world, and wrapping up his moral observations in little tabloid packages, to improve posterity. The miracle, I repeat, is that this most capacious and artistic of human minds should have been vouchsafed to us in the person of a common player who, with all the limitations that station, education, language, and vocation put upon him, should none the less have achieved the most imperishable fame among those who have dealt with the magic of the written word.

The Return to Shakespearean Orthodoxy

Of the making of books on Shakespeare there is never an end. Nor is an end likely, because as time goes on, more and more are interested in this greatest among creative minds, and the slender facts and records of which we can be certain suffuse an atmosphere of mystery and excite that far from the least noble of human proclivities, the urge to the making of myths. No man who has attracted the attention of his fellows in great number has ever escaped the penumbra of myth, whether it brighten by contrast the nimbus of his glory or darken it with the shadows of detraction. So that he who deals with the greatness of a Homer, a Tiberius, a Dante, or a Napoleon is involved at once in questions of distinction between the close march of facts and the untrammeled flights of fancy. Another human proclivity further complicates historical and biographical investigation, and that is an equally human reluctance to acknowledge the limitations of our own powers of observation and deduction, the itch to leave nothing unexplained; and there are few who do not prefer the rôle of the prophet, or wise man at least, to the discouraging attitude of the agnostic. Comment on Shakespeare, with much that is excellent, has long suffered from both of these tendencies, and we have had, in the extremes, the exploitation of what is little better than mere scandal and, on the other hand, the effort ingeniously to explain away every difficulty and pad the absence of evidence with plausible conjecture.

Orthodoxy is, be it confessed, no very accurate term to employ as to the findings of science or even as to those of history. But there is, in the growth of opinion and scholarship on any topic, a middle way between timorous acceptance and eccentric theorizing, a middle way that keeps steadily on, absorbing to itself after considered scrutiny such progress as can be made by the unearthing of new material or by a wiser understanding of what we have. It is in this sense that I employ the word "orthodoxy," which has here to do with the trend of critical opinion as to Shakespeare and his work, and the turn which criticism has taken of late towards an estimate less imaginative, less eccentric, if less certain of its findings, an estimate alike conservative, considered, and fair.

The variety of Shakespearean investigation is endless: there is obviously biography which is always with us, the archeology of the age, the topography of Elizabethan Stratford and London, stage history, so far as we can reconstruct it, the environment of Shakespeare in every use and misuse of that word, and, coming to the dramas themselves, there are endless bibliographical, textual, metrical and other questions, questions of the limits of authorship and collaboration, of authenticity, of origin and influences, of printing, proofreading, now even of handwriting. Have we six or seven signatures of Shakespeare? on which nice matter depends the allegation of his one-time ownership of a copy of Montaigne's *Essays,* now in the British Museum, and much by way of inference as to his reading. Was he a well man or palsied when he signed his will? Have we or have we not a transcription in his own hand of the whole scene of a play on Sir Thomas More, the joint production of several playwrights, according to a familiar Elizabethan custom? The reading of the recent summary of this single problem in Shakespearean authorship, as set forth with its prodigious array of bibliography by Sir Edmund Chambers, will alone convince the layman of the extraordinary vitality and exuberance of contemporary Shakespeare scholarship.[1] The elucidation of this question involves niceties of date, intricacies of stage history, quality of content, style, and above all the identification of the handwriting of several Elizabethan playwrights. To this end—as in a great criminal trial—the expert and would-be expert have been invoked, and one indefatigable American scholar has brought to bear upon it the artillery of a whole new science—that of "bibliotics," as it was named years ago by its inventor, the late Dr. Persifor Frazer of Philadelphia.[2] The question from its very nature must remain undecided, though there are many who would fain agree—all the minutiae of the experts to the contrary notwithstanding—that in more than one scene of this composite drama, the tone and spirit, the realization of character, the vocabulary in the coupling of words, even a certain characteristic playing with them—all these things are consistent with Shakespeare, and less in the manner of any other contemporary dramatist.

In a paper of any reasonable scope we cannot attempt even a bare recital of recent activities in Shakespeare scholarship and criticism. Let us take three or four typical works of genuine scholarship to note in them an evident reaction which emphatically calls for a reappraisal of the scanty facts which are ascertainable as to Shakespeare and his work, and for a halt upon those safer premises, alike of the destructive criticism which calls everything into doubt and the method of surmise which erects on the ruins of probability structures often perilous and absurd. Two such books are those of Pro-

[1] See the whole discussion in E. K. Chambers, *William Shakespeare*, I, 499–515.

[2] *Bibliotics or the Study of Documents, Determination of Individual Character of Handwriting, etc.*, 1901.

fessor Pierce Butler and of John S. Smart;[3] and in both the stress is specifically on a return, simple and honest, to the materials, the data, the facts on which to rebuild a safer and a sounder biography of Shakespeare. The recent studies of Edgar I. Fripp and Sir Edmund Chambers,[4] involving this as well, enter, the one more deeply, in a continuation of the author's previous researches into the minute relations and details of Shakespeare's Stratford and the people who were his family's contemporaries there; while the other, in two fine volumes, brings to a triumphant completion this indefatigable scholar's long-continued studies in the many, and often vexed, problems which arise not only out of what we know of Shakespeare's life, but out of his work under the conditions to which he was subjected.

The books of Professor Butler and the late Dr. Smart offer an interesting contrast of the manner in which two scholars, working quite independently in a field already gleaned and garnered apparently to the last straw, can throw none the less each a new light on many a point and come to a substantial agreement by different ways. Professor Butler's book is particularly valuable in its assembly into a sizable volume of the significant anecdotes, "lives," criticisms, and documents relating to Shakespeare; and for the quiet hand of an unobtrusive guidance to the understanding of them. Here are the familiar allusions that we know so well, and those which we have taken for granted time out of mind, each referred to its source and its place in the category that goes to make up what we may confidently affirm that we "know about Shakespeare"; and neither con-

[3] *Materials for the Life of Shakespeare*, 1930; *Shakespeare, Truth and Tradition*, 1928.

[4] *Shakespeare Studies*, 1930; *William Shakespeare, a Study of Facts and Problems*, 2 vols., 1930.

troversy nor, much less, any theorizing is allowed to interfere with the plain unvarnished tale. Here is Dr. Butler's comment on Shakespeare's quest for his father's achievement of a coat of arms: "Thus, like half a dozen other actors, including members of his own company, Burbage and Heming, Shakespeare had a recognized and not an outcast status." And once more, as to the dramatist's testimony in the Mountjoy lawsuit in 1612—the interesting discovery, it will be remembered, of our American scholar, the late Dr. C. W. Wallace: "Different readers will read different things between the lines of this testimony—perhaps it is not going too far to say that Shakespeare's testimony seems reluctant, as if he would not further contribute to a domestic quarrel, as if he would remember only the amiable things about either Belott or Mountjoy." [5]

Dr. Smart's book is more argumentative and, while employing the documents with equal fullness and frankness, discusses them less as such. Where the American critic proceeds from the earlier biographies and anecdotes to contemporary criticism and personal relations, concluding with the evidences as to the plays, the Scotsman—to designate Dr. Smart's nationality accurately—proceeds from Stratford and family history to an active combat with error in his entertaining chapter on "Things Which Never Were"; and he does not even disdain to cross swords with the Shakespearean heretics, now long since out of date, who mix up Francis Bacon with the authorship of stage plays. In view of the several more recent heresies which have followed this old Victorian wraith, it seems a pity to waste so much wit and energy on so dead a topic. But as a piece of clever writing and sound *reductio ad absurdum,* Dr. Smart's lively chapter, "The Strange Conspiracy," is heartily to be commended. I

[5] Butler, *op. cit.,* pp. 104 and 148.

like, too, among the "fragments," the dictum: "Shakespeare might have written as carelessly as Byron, and as illegibly as Dean Stanley or Andrew Lang, and might still be the author of *Hamlet";* and the turn given to that old scandal, Shakespeare's bequeathal of his "second-best bed" to his wife, with a parallel from Mr. Arnold Bennett's novel, *The Old Wives' Tale,* by which it appears that when a certain widow returned to visit the young couple, her daughter and her daughter's husband, who had inherited the estate, "she was not asked to occupy the second best room like Mrs. Shakespeare, that being her place as a dowager [but was actually installed,] as a great concession and a special act of courtesy, . . . in the best, which had formerly been her own." [6]

All four of the books under discussion in these paragraphs agree in repudiating the idea of a dirty and illiterate Stratford, a father for Shakespeare who could neither read nor write, and a poet handicapped with a pitiful unacquaintance not only with the classics, but with anything else that makes for culture or learning. But the other extreme—once so ingeniously sponsored by Churton Collins—that the dramatist was a considerable linguist, stepping from passage to passage of the Greek dramatists and the Latin satirists or lyrists with the ease and unoriginality of an Oxford don, is quite as equally repudiated. Dr. Smart raises a number of interesting questions as to this matter of the education of genius, in which he reminds us that "Keats received what education he possessed in a private school, where he learned no Greek," that Dickens received an even scantier education than Keats, that "George Meredith knew nothing of Universities," and that "Thomas Hardy spent his boyhood in elementary schools in country places." And, recalling that men have

[6] *Shakespeare, Truth and Tradition,* p. 213.

been graduates of both Universities, as Robert Greene, Shakespeare's early rival, was given to boasting, and have taken precious little learning away with them, he neatly turns the tables by asking: Do we really *know* that Shakespeare was not a University man? concluding: "There were many students duly entered at a College and in residence there who neither matriculated nor graduated. A complete list of Cambridge students is only to be obtained by working through the Admissions Registers of all the Colleges." And after citing the instance of Oliver Cromwell, who was admitted to Sidney Sussex in 1616 and resided there for a year, but did not matriculate or graduate, he declares: "Until the archives of the Colleges for the appropriate dates have been minutely searched and no William Shakespeare discovered, it will be impossible to prove from University sources that he was never at Oxford [or Cambridge] even for a term." [7]

Even more pertinent to the question is Mr. Fripp's surprising chapter, "Shakespeare's Use of Ovid's *Metamorphoses,*" in which he shows that our glib acceptance of Arthur Golding's "clownish translation" as the source for the many reminiscences and quotations from Ovid to be found scattered up and down Shakespeare's plays, is preposterous.[8] He further shows that many more such reminiscences than we have ever suspected—and these he gives in full—go to prove that Shakespeare knew his schoolbook, as he should after seven years at an excellent Latin school, his Ovid in the original, and what is more to the purpose, "*loved* it." We may add that he assiduously used it, with a surprising verbal nicety and accuracy.

Mr. Fripp's Shakespearean studies range widely, and this is no

[7] Smart, *op. cit.,* pp. 175 ff.

[8] *Shakespeare Studies,* 1904, pp. 98 ff.

less than the fourth book from his fertile and ready pen. As was to be expected from *Shakespeare's Stratford* and *Master Richard Quyny,* previous volumes, the present work is strong in antiquarian research as to the fellow townsmen of the dramatist. Where all is so interesting, it is difficult to specify. "The Minister Who Baptized Shakespeare," John Bretchgirdle, and "John Brownsword: Poet and Schoolmaster," to whom Shakespeare must have gone to school, are pertinent and full of new and absorbingly interesting material. Later the subjects range from "Light on Doctor Hall," who married Shakespeare's daughter, to "Monsieur Jaques," which the present writer confesses that he cannot follow, and an exceedingly illuminating paper on Falstaff, immortal theme for the wise and the merely intrepid. Amongst innumerable smaller matters, Mr. Fripp shows that John Shakespeare's "difficulties" towards the end of his life were not Roman Catholic recusancy, as some have thought, but perhaps too warm a sympathy in the opposite extreme. It is good also to have another example of the word "aroint" which occurs, always as applied to a witch ("aroint thee"), in both *Macbeth* and *King Lear:* and this time from a bit of contemporary Stratford testimony recorded by Dr. Hall, bringing this strange word in the Shakespearean vocabulary singularly near home.[9]

The "biography" of Shakespeare, to leave it for more important things, has been written, rewritten, and miswritten to a frazzle. Not a guess has been unguessed or a distortion undistorted. And yet, to quote the words of the very latest writer upon him, "Shakespeare, the man, is transparent and inscrutable"; in a word, the outward life of Shakespeare is quite the least important thing about him. For,

[9] *Ibid., passim.* The quotation of the word "aroint" or "arent thee, witch!" is presented on p. 170.

unlike many lesser men who can hold up the mirror of their art only before their own petty personalities, here was a master who achieved that detachment, that oblivion of self in which alone can any art hope to reach a universal significance.

To turn to Sir Edmund Chambers' *William Shakespeare, a Study of Facts and Problems,* we are in the presence of a singularly complete and exhaustive piece of criticism and research. For in these two handsome volumes the author brings to conclusion the ambition and the study of a lifetime. Realizing that no man's career nor any series of happenings can be viewed except in the light of the fullest possible understanding of his age and his personal surroundings, Sir Edmund began his purposed work on Shakespeare more than thirty years ago, with the publication of that fascinating book, *The Mediaeval Stage,*[10] thus clearing up the origins of the drama in England. Years after came the four scholarly volumes on *The Elizabethan Stage,* which summarized, with critical distinction and in orderly arrangement, the learning which has gathered during generations as to the theatrical background of Shakespeare, his contemporaries, their plays, the manner of their writing, and the conditions of the time as affecting all this. And now the author is at last ready for the central figure of his long-prepared labors, Shakespeare himself. There are two ways of writing history, and biography as well. The aim of one is the production of a picture to visualize, so to speak, in the imagination, the subject that the reader may *see.* The other seeks the perfection of a map, that the reader may be sure to *find his way,* and leaves "seeing" to the reader's own eyes. For the average reader—and we are most of us such—the picture is impera-

[10] Two volumes, printed in 1903; *The Elizabethan Stage,* four volumes, appeared twenty years later.

tive, for he can see only what is visualized for him. For the scholar the guidance of the map is not only alone sufficient; he often resents the other method. In view of this distinction, it will not be taken as captious in us to recognize that these splendid volumes of Chambers' are essentially for the student who cannot bring too much scholarship to the understanding of them, and he cannot be sufficiently grateful for this orderly, sound, and complete presentation of a subject the intricacy of which it would be difficult to exaggerate.

It may not be remembered by all that the text of Shakespeare's plays as we read it today in modern editions is the result of the study, the correction, the emendation of some seven or eight generations of scholars; for while, contrary to popular opinion, most of the early editions of these plays, individually or collectively, were not really very bad according to the standards of the time or indeed of any time, it is equally true that there are many places in which there is need, not only of the specific knowledge, but of the application of that species of genius that goes alike to the attainment of truth whether it be in the discovery of a new chemical property or in the restitution to integrity of a poetical figure overlaid by a misprint. But the activity of scholars, here as elsewhere, has not stopped at a restitution of the text. It has gone further, as in the Homeric question or in matters appertaining to the text of the Bible itself, to doubt, to question, and to disintegrate, sometimes with adequate and interesting results, at times with a stubborn skepticism that seems begotten far more of egotism and a desire for the distinction of singularity than of the scholar's love of truth. It is impossible here to do more than suggest the nature of some of the many problems of text and authorship with which this encyclopedic work is concerned. For example, there is a no more vexed or difficult question than that which concerns the history of the stage in the age of Shakespeare: the facts by way of record are scattered and incomplete; the companies were many and confused, alike in their patrons and their personnel, both of which were open to incessant change, shifting, coalition, division, appearance now at Court, again in London, and fitfully in the provinces.[11] Contrary to the neat theories of the late Sir Sidney Lee and others, which trace Shakespeare as a boy attracted by the Earl of Leicester's theatrical entertainments at Kenilworth into the orbit of the players, Sir Edmund, in agreement with Adams, finds Shakespeare's emergence as a player and playwright in the theatrical disorganization of the years 1592 to 1594, circumspectly admitting the alternatives of an association with Pembroke's men, with Sussex's, or even the status of an unattached playwright.[12] And he rejects another recent surmise which reconstructs for Shakespeare a regular period of seven years' apprenticeship, and ties him to a system in which his art was largely determined by the personalities and the limitations of his players.[13] On the more solid ground which follows, our knowledge of Shakespeare as "a payee on behalf of the Chamberlain's men for plays given at court in the winter of 1594," we progress forward rapidly in the familiar story of the dramatist's career, coming again and again upon adjudications or *obiter dicta* which illuminate the theses or refute the arguments of less governed scholarship.

One of our prevalent departures into the realms of allusive fancy, where historical analogies exist in the atmosphere of a world of four

[11] Chambers, *Life of Shakespeare,* II, p. 295.

[12] S. Lee, *Life of Shakespeare,* ed. 1925, and Chambers, as above, I, 56, 94; also J. Q. Adams, *Life of Shakespeare,* p. 130.

[13] T. W. Baldwin, *The Organization and Personnel of the Shakespearean Company,* 1927.

dimensions, transforms Shakespeare's dramatic transcripts of history and story into deeply planned allegories of contemporary or recent Elizabethan events. According to this species of twist as to the significance of things, it will be remembered that Hamlet becomes an adumbration of King James before his accession to his English throne, and the story of his mother, Mary Queen of Scots, and Bothwell is set forth in that of Macbeth and his lady. Here is our author's wholesome verdict as to that sort of thing: "I do not myself believe that, apart from some passages of obvious satire in comic scenes, there is much of the topical in Shakespeare, whose mind normally moved upon quite another plane of relation to life." [14]

An absorbing and informing chapter of this work is that entitled "The Book of the Play," the phrase employed contemporaneously to denote not the author's manuscript or "original," but that manuscript as ordered, corrected, and otherwise arranged to guide the prompter or "bookkeeper" in his direction of the play. Scholarship of late has been very active in this matter of Elizabethan dramatic manuscripts, of which an interesting variety—though, alas, perhaps none certainly of Shakespeare's—is extant; [15] and the work of Greg, Sisson, Sir Edmund, and many others has made many of these accessible and has studied them with illuminating results to our knowledge of things, extending from the handwriting of the period, as suggested above, to the possible effects of manuscript peculiarities and imperfections on the text of plays subsequently in print. In its

[14] See L. Winstanley, *Hamlet and the Scottish Succession,* 1921; *Macbeth, King Lear and Contemporary History,* 1922; E. Rickert, "Political Propaganda . . . in the Essex Conspiracy," *Modern Philology,* 1923; or E. M. Albright, "Shakespeare and the Essex Conspiracy," *Publications of the Modern Language Association,* 1927.

[15] See A. Harbage, "Elizabethan and Seventeenth Century Play," MSS., *ibid.,* L, 501, 1935.

wider reaches this is a subject of great intricacy, involving, as it does with much else, that maze of difficulty, the Elizabethan practice of collaboration in playwriting. Of late years a theory has been evolved, especially in the hands of Dr. J. Dover Wilson, one of the learned editors of the *New Cambridge Shakespeare,* by which—to express the idea somewhat by way of exaggeration—a species of "continuous copy" is surmised as having existed in the possession of the theatrical company, begun originally by one or more writers and open to a succession of subsequent rewritings and revisions at the hands of apparently anybody who might be employed temporarily for the purpose.[16] Such a theory, in the upshot, transforms Shakespeare, with most of his fellows, into a mere "play-patcher," mending and amending, without original or artistic purpose or design; and arrogates, on the part of a critic such as Mr. J. M. Robertson for example, a preternatural discernment into the niceties of vocabulary, diction, and the use of figure by which these writers of three hundred years since are delicately to be distinguished.[17] Sir Edmund, as might have been expected from his brilliant lecture on "The Disintegration of Shakespeare"[18] a few years since, will have none of this; and a general vindication of the Shakespearean text from every point of view is not the least valuable of the many services of this book.

To these paragraphs may perhaps not unaptly be added a word as to the newer trend of the study of the bibliography of earlier English books, which has given to us such admirable works as *A Short-Title Catalogue of Books Printed in England between 1475 and*

[16] See the various Introductions to *The New Cambridge Shakespeare,* and especially *The Manuscript of Hamlet,* 2 vols., 1934.

[17] *The Shakespeare Canon,* 1932.

[18] Reprinted in *Aspects of Shakespeare,* 1933.

1640, the scholarly compilation of Messrs. A. W. Pollard and G. R. Redgrave with the help of many others, 1926; R. B. McKerrow's *Introduction to Bibliography,* 1927; and now Percy Simpson's *Proof-Reading in the Sixteenth, Seventeenth and Eighteenth Centuries,* 1935, a work of a fine thoroughness. All of these shed light upon Shakespearean publication, as on so much else, systematizing and appraising where much was guess and surmise, and doing away with many a superstition of the older methods of the repetition of authority for that thorough and complete scrutiny on the basis of which alone can anything like scientific accuracy be founded. This last monumental work was preceded by two very interesting contributions to information as to the processes by which the plays of Shakespeare came into print. The one, Professor Tucker Brooke's note in *Elizabethan Proof Corrections, in a Copy of "The First Part of the Contentions, 1600";* the second, E. E. Willoughby's extensive examination into the circumstances of *The Printing of the First Folio of Shakespeare.*[19] In the first of these we have before us, reproduced from specimens in the Huntington Collection, "the actual pages read by the corrector . . . and given to the compositor as revised proof of the play in question," involving no less than a score of distinct changes; in Mr. Willoughby's inquiry are printed in facsimile a page of the folio of *Antony and Cleopatra,* showing the original proof-corrections, and the original [type] setting of the final pages of *Romeo and Juliet* and the first page of *Troilus and Cressida.* Without here going into minutiae ill suited to a cursory survey such as this, we may rejoice in repeating with Mr. Willoughby: "There is no reason . . . to believe that the compositors and proof-readers of the First Folio introduced any great corruption into the text," and

[19] These books date 1929 and 1930.

strengthen this final overthrow of the much-mooted theory of the inferiority of the Shakespearean text with the words of Mr. Simpson, who adds: "Altogether, the corrections which are made [in the text of the First Folio], indicate the normal standard of a personal corrector," whose workmanship may not improperly be designated as "moderately careful but not meticulous." Without pursuing this interesting summary of the books which mark, in Shakespeare scholarship, a return to reasonableness and orthodoxy, I may conclude that we are looking forward to the early publication of a work examining exhaustively the texts of the three folios that followed the first with reference to the editorial supervision actually bestowed upon them. By this it will appear that each of the folios actually received in its day an attention in the printing and handling of the text far more careful, if not actually scholarly, than the long-accepted theories on this subject have been willing to admit.[20]

[20] See the forthcoming volume of Doctors Black and Shaaber, *Editorial Changes in Second, Third and Fourth Folios of Shakespeare.*

Shakespeare Our Contemporary

THERE is a charming thought, somewhere, of Charles Lamb's in which he declares his preference for the reading of old poets in their original, uncompromising, ponderous folios. The weight of the book, the difficulty of the old lettering, the ancient sheep's binding fallen into partial decay, even the occasional little tunnels of the industrious bookworm—all these things add to the flavor of antiquity which proclaims Chaucer or Spenser, Beaumont and Fletcher or Doctor Donne beings of another, an earlier and now somewhat antiquated world. But when this literary epicure turns to Shakespeare, he tells us: "I like the editions of him best, which have been oftenest tumbled about and handled"; in a word, he prefers his Shakespeare in modern dress, dress possibly as modern and sumptuous as you like. For Shakespeare is of Lamb's day, or my day, as much as he was of his own and is of all other days. In Ben Jonson's familiar words: "He was not of an age, but for all time," and thus is best viewed by the average reader from the vantage of that reader's particular moment. Accepting this nice distinction of the gentle Elia as to Shakespeare in contrast with others of our earlier poets and dramatists, I should like to add: In the volume of Shakespeare from which I read, let the print be large and black and unornamental, adapted to eyes that have read not wisely but too much; and secondly, let there be illustrations neither of Lear at his maddest nor of Sir Andrew Aguecheek at his silliest—illustrations, however excellent and artistic, that mix up my Shakespeare with the Shakespeare of some other man, however capable he may be with brush or pencil.

For a generation or more it has been my privilege to read Shakespeare with mature students for hours every week. I recall a couple of years in which I so read the tragedies in Philadelphia, the comedies in New York—why, I do not know, unless that the latter were better fitted to the levity of Broadway. And as to some things I became more and more impressed. Among them is the grip that Shakespeare gets on the modern young man and woman, when actually read and not merely talked about; and secondly the amazing applicability of the Shakespearean reading of life to our life of today, if we will only read aright, that is to say, if we will seek humbly to ascertain the poet's actual meaning and not read into him your sense or my sense, which, let us frankly confess, is often little better than nonsense.

We who are given over to books are prone to think of Shakespeare only too commonly in antiquarian terms. We study the topography of Bohemia, especially its seacoast, and we are strong in the landscape gardening of Belmont. We should never make the mistake of sending Shylock on the stage with a white or even a red turban, for we know —wise ones that we are—that, being a Levantine Jew, his hat or turban should be orange-tawny. And we smile with indulgent superiority when we hear that David Garrick acted Macbeth in the scarlet coat and gold lace of a contemporary British major general. When we stage Shakespeare nowadays, we usually follow what we think was the actual Elizabethan staging of his plays, thereby perpetuating an interesting anachronism but one more or less abortive and barren. We find ourselves, almost before we know it, making allowances for the limitations, as we call them, of the Shakespearean art, his superstitions and old wives' tales, and patronizing the poet for the one irreparable misfortune of his existence and its awful consequences, that he did not live in a time just like ours, in a city precisely like our own, inhabited by amiable people exactly like ourselves.

If there is anything certain about what has been called the temperament of Shakespeare, it is the assurance which we have of his absolute contemporaneousness. He was not a medieval man like Spenser, weaving a beautiful and useless tapestry of times long gone, in a charming pattern repeated and repeated with the persistency of wall paper. And he was not a classically minded man, like Ben Jonson, who knew that the ancients had done everything far better than we and that any time not spent in imitating them should be employed in bewailing our deplorable inferiority. There are men who have failed in a given age because they came before their time; they were out of joint with their day and died misunderstood. There are men, on the other hand, who are out of joint with the time because they cannot keep up with it, strive how they may. I once heard of a man who spent so much of his time in hunting up precedents—an occupation best accomplished by walking backward—that by the time he died he had nearly caught up with his grandfather. Now Shakespeare was not like any of these, nor did he ever waste his time in trying to convince anybody by argument about anything. What he did when he came up to London was to set about becoming a good actor, a quick and able mender of old plays, and a clever imitator of Lyly for light rapid dialogue and of Marlowe for passionate tragedy full of poetry, while his savings went back into the company. Shakespeare, in a word, was an unusually practical and adaptable man. His business capacity is unquestionable; not the kind that follows only what other people are doing, but the kind that supplies better goods and raises the standard of the output, to speak in the parlance of factories. There came a time when he led his profession; but he never led it out of the normal, rational path of its development artistically or commercially, for he was as sanely imaginative in business as in poetry, and able to divine what was coming and to ride comfortably on the crest of contemporary success, guiding public taste in the process and creating new wants in the gratification of them.

A certain New York manager was approached some years ago with a proposition that he take advantage of the tercentenary year of the death of Shakespeare to stage some of the great dramatist's plays as an honor to the poet's memory and a possible emolument to himself. But, immersed in the trivialities of musical comedy and the banalities of things worse, he is said to have replied: "Shakespeare! Bosh! Shakespeare has been dead three hundred years, let us keep him so." In less than a month after, the city of New York raised a handsome guarantee fund for a season commemorative of the great poet. Whereupon this same manager saw the light and sought eagerly to take over the management of precisely the thing which he had so recently damned. There were men like this in Shakespeare's day; they are always with us. But Shakespeare was not of that ilk; he was no mere follower in the wake of the public and of the opinions of other men. In his youth he occasionally wrote down to the lower levels of his auditors. In his maturity he rarely sins in this way; for such condescensions he must instinctively have felt are in the nature of artistic insincerity, in which lies the sacrifice of the dramatist's morale and ultimately the grave of all veritable art.

As a manager, we may feel sure that Shakespeare would have welcomed every new device that could make the drama more effective. Better lighting, more striking and elaborate scenery though not to the degree of destroying the artistic effect, mechanical appliances, costume reasonably adapted to the locus of the play—all these things he would eagerly have adopted; although I hesitate to believe that he might not have balked at the form of quasi-theatrical entertainment which for many years substituted a mingled torture and titillation of the eye for the glories of sound, sense, and genuine emotion and even now often slaughters all these things to a veritable glut of the senses, dulled the while by the incessant pounding rhythm that masks under the name of incidental music. Shakespeare would have laughed at the superstition that regards every line of a play of his as sacrosanct; and he would have welcomed cutting, addition, and adaptation to new needs made by competent hands. He would have delighted in the artistic photography that presents the scenes, for example, of his dream of a midsummer night's fairyland, with a grace, beauty, and artistic inventiveness that only his own great imagination could transcend; although I question if he might approve the slipping back of his conception of dainty, genial, sympathetic Puck into a gross hoydenish Lob-lie-by-the-fire, strident of voice, gesticulatory, vulgar, discordant, a realization of the unilluminated fidelity of Ben Jonson to countryside tradition, not Shakespeare's delicate imaginative art. Accustomed in his time only to a squeaking boyish Cleopatra and a male Lady Macbeth of years at most fourteen, Shakespeare would enthusiastically have welcomed women to his stage to take his choice and precious women's parts, giving them credit in the "quality" which he himself professed for that superiority over his own ruder sex which, in his fidelity to truth, he bestows on womanhood throughout his plays. I sometimes wonder what Shakespeare might have thought concerning women in public life as we see, or at least at some time have seen some of them. Ben Jonson thought about the enfranchised woman and wrote about her not amiably, and so did an unhappy Puritan named William Prynne, losing his ears in the pillory for his temerity in lampooning the sex. But Shakespeare is silent on this score, though feminine capability to manage her own affairs, and the affairs as well of most of the men about her, is not wanting to the Portias, the Rosalinds, and the Beatrices of his plays; and assuredly neither Cleopatra nor Lady Macbeth, before her woman's heartstrings broke under the strain, was wanting in any of the capabilities which we so celebrate today. Shakespeare, indeed, is often remarkable for what he leaves unsaid and unexpressed. His was the soul of discretion. It has been constantly noted that one cannot make out Shakespeare's theological creed nor the political party to which he belonged. These are greater uncertainties about him than where he was schooled or of what disease he died. There is extant, as everyone knows, a coat of arms of the Shakespeares. But there is no need of such evidences. Shakespeare's reticences as well as his utterances proclaim him ever the gentleman.

But I return to Shakespeare's contemporaneousness. With all his minor difficulties, Shakespeare is really the most intelligible of all the poets; and that is because he is still speaking to us in a language, with a spirit and in an attitude towards all the great essentials of life and conduct, which is perennially fresh and contemporary. There are three thousand five hundred palpable printer's errors in the first folio edition of his plays: at least the critics, who wander much in error and must know all about it, tell us so. And yet the layman can follow the general trend of Shakespeare's thought with ease and pleasure without the corrections, emendations, suggestions, and impertinences which scholarship and would-be scholarship have lavished upon him. There are hundreds of allusions to matters of custom, manners, dress, decorum, arts, games, and modes of speech, which we can grasp only by means of notes if we are fully to understand them. And yet we are in no doubt as to the conduct of any one of these plays or as to the trend of any of their dialogue. There are a thousand personages in these dramas, from those charged with intricate and difficult speaking parts to those that appear no more than by name; and yet each personality is readily grasped in the larger essentials by him who reads, if not by him who runs. There are sentiments that arise out of hundreds of situations in these plays, from those that move the lightest and most trivial laughter to moments of pause before the mysteries of life, crime, death, and eternity, to each of which we yield an instinctive assent, because it affirms a truth that finds echo in the heart of each of us. And there are scores of passages in which—if you are in your nature a true and not a seeming man or woman—you will humbly confess that here is a philosophy, a guidance, a justice, a large toleration infinitely above your own. These are some of the things in which we recognize Shakespeare our contemporary, things that keep him in some respects as yet well in advance of this cruel, backward, lagging world of ours.

A conspicuous feature, an all but unexampled one, is this prevailing modernity in Shakespeare. Neither Homer nor Vergil nor Dante nor Milton shares it. And when we mention lesser men, Pope, Wordsworth, Shelley; in the wider reaches of the drama, Corneille, even Calderon, Dryden, Goethe, Ibsen and, with a leap forward and downward, our sometime very contemporary George Bernard Shaw—how much was each the creature of his age! Modernity, if we would but understand things aright, is not the invention of something absolutely new and undreamed in the hallucinations of our ancestors. Modernity is rather the continuance of a tried tradition in things which are really worth while, the recognition of universal truths in their applications whether to one age or to all. People of fashion in all ages are concerned with externals and trivialities, the mode of dress, manners at table or in salutation, the prevalence of a given game or diversion, the slang of the passing moment which you must know as to the manner born or you are a creature of the outer darkness. These matters as they touch his age we have to study when we read Shakespeare or we are shocked that Hamlet, a prince, should throw himself down on the rushes at the feet of Ophelia in the Court of Denmark and bandy a kind of small talk with her that would count him today a boor. But when we turn to the essentials, the valor of men, the purity of woman, the deadliness of injustice not only to those who are the victims of it but to those who themselves inflict it, when we turn to the obligations of oaths, the essential nobility of man, all said and done, and to the need of a larger charity in this world if we are to look for charity for our own frailties—in those things Shakespeare is as sound today and as uplifting as he was in his own time and, for aught that we can imagine to the contrary, such he will continue to be when the pyramids are a thousand years older.

It is, then, as a modern, a contemporary, a poet with a fresh vision and a certain guidance that I would have Shakespeare read today. The old Greek dramatists would have welcomed him as a brother, seeing with eyes as clear as their own. The cultivated Roman would have rejoiced in Shakespeare's practical wisdom and ease in dealing with the affairs of the world. Chaucer would have delighted in his humor, at its best the only match for his own. It was only the captious and pharisaical age of criticism that called the Shakespearean supremacy into question and impertinently rewrote him; for to narrow, dry, ingrowing provincialism Shakespeare must always seem alien and difficult. He was adored in his own spacious times, a certain truth that cannot be repeated too often. And it argues well for the essential taste, the liberality and the soundness of the judgment of our own time that, whether we reason into confusion his ethics or his art, his psychology or his ideals, as not precisely identical with all the little idols of these things that we have fashioned for ourselves, Shakespeare is still accepted popularly and universally as the world's greatest dramatist and poet: when all has been said, the greatest, with no very good second.

The Land That the Puritans Put Behind Them

As to Puritans, I have opinions of my own, which I need not ventilate here at large as my theme is happily not Puritanism. Two words, however, and we may disembark from the *Mayflower*. The English Puritans were a righteous and a stiff-necked people. Under stress of persecution they split, some abandoning England, some remaining to fight the Parliamentary battles of Hampton and Pym and arm the Ironsides of Cromwell. It cannot be affirmed that the Puritans made any advance towards even a measurable toleration of opinions other than their own; nor can it be maintained that, in their age and time of power, the Puritans exercised any monopoly in the persecution either of themselves or of others. It is, too, to be observed that the Puritans were not always what they afterwards became. Spenser was a Puritan in a sense, as well as Milton, and as well, if not with the same emphasis, as Cotton Mather or Jonathan Edwards. In short, the Puritans de-liberalized steadily under difficulties. We might say that something happened to the sweet Elizabethan milk of human kindness, with its rich cream of the joy of life rising to the brim. Perhaps it was the religious storms of the age that turned it to a species of bonnyclabber, and the Puritans were the whey which time drew off, acidulated and thin. But it is for us to look not backward to stern, militant Geneva nor forward to rockbound inhospitable New England, but to that older England and some of its characteristics, its worldly fascinations, its intellectual ideals and achievements which made the Puritan abandonment of their native country an act of heroic renunciation.

It was a tight little island that the Puritan fathers put behind them. Of a population less than that of our present Pennsylvania, England was then possessed of but one city of any size, that of London; and London scarcely numbered two hundred thousand souls when the colonization of New England began. It was still a walled, a medieval town, dominated by the Tower, a fortress traditionally of Julius Caesar's founding; and its streets, lined with peaked and timbered houses, were narrow and tortuous and unpaved. You walked dry-shod only close to the houses, and many were the quarrels that arose, often involving the drawing of blood as well as of swords, to avoid a thrust into the kennel, as the central gutter was called. The houses abutting closer in the upper stories, left but an irregular ribbon of blue, or rather gray, sky overhead. On the other hand, in Elizabethan London few houses were without gardens, to the rear at least, and the liberties—a London word perpetuated in our Philadelphia Liberties of Southwark, Spring Garden and the like—contained many walks and commons, the enjoyment of which was among the inalienable rights of the citizens. Nothing strikes the reader of our old literature more favorably than the English love of flowers, of gardens, and of the countryside. Shakespeare is full of it; and even formal, worldly Bacon unbends to gardens. The Elizabethans lived much out of doors. The popular Shakespearean theatre was open to the sky, and there was much resort to open places, even in cities. There were, too, hunting, fishing, hawking, archery and the other rural sports, such as those of Mayday: circling about the Puritan-despised Maypole, dancing, revels, masquerades, riding at tilt, and tournaments. There were sports less noble: that of bull-baiting and of bear-baiting, in which a bear, such as old Sackerson, was tied blindfold to a stake and set upon by fighting mastiffs. You will remember how silly Master Slender boasts in *The Merry Wives* of his fearlessness of that beast to Mistress Anne Page. Admirable old Roger Ascham, grave tutor to Queen Elizabeth, wrote a treatise on the then gentleman's sport of cockfighting, a work unhappily now lost; and there was much betting at bowls, tennis, and football, a well-known Elizabethan game, not nearly so dangerous as it has become since in America. Shakespeare bids Cleopatra, somewhere, to a game of billiards. And there were more dangerous games even than Cleopatra's. I own a seventeenth-century book entitled *The Complete Gamester,* which is so fascinating in its reprobation and relish of every species of the game of chance, that I prudently lock it up from the very young. But we are wandering far away from the Puritan.

There was abundance of good cheer in the England that the Puritans put behind them: the tables of the merchant, the farmer, and even the artisan groaned with variety, especially of meats, of fish and game, succeeded by marchpanes, puddings, venison and other pasties and what not; and, added to honest English ale, were many foreign and sophisticated wines, like Falstaff's sherris-sack, and stronger waters such as Irish usquebaugh, now spelled whiskey. The books of the day accuse these foreign importations of bringing about a degree of inebriety not known in earlier good old English days. It is always the foreigner who corrupts us; I am sure that you have observed this: we really have no vices of our own. I do not wish to be unfair, but I cannot find that the Puritans left England from any provident desire to avoid overeating, however a beneficent Providence added fasting in New England to prayer. It is a delicate question, but I do not think either that it was from an overwhelming urge to experiment in prohibition prophetically, so to speak, that the Puritans left England. Like most other people, our Puritan forbears do not appear to have disapproved of many a thing so much because of the thing itself, as because of the glaring circumstance that the "other fellow" was doing it. For example, a doughty champion of moral earnestness and Puritan discipline once wrote a book *On the Unloveliness of Lovelocks.* A lovelock was a harmless wisp of hair which the young gallants of the age allowed to curl in graceful sinuosities over the forehead, tickling the nose and impeding the sight; for the cavalier, as we all remember, wore his hair long, and the roundhead was so called because he didn't. Terrible was the invective hurled against this wicked cavalier practice of the wearing of lovelocks, its vanity, its plain trespass against divine law. But do you suppose for a moment that, if the cavalier had cropped his head and the Puritan had not done so, we should have failed of a corresponding invective, equally eloquent, against the idolatrous shears that the abandoned cavalier employed to clip the hair that Providence had ordained should grow long upon the head of man? Little could the Puritan father have foreseen to what a degree his feminine descendants were destined to follow his example; how much they were to crop off of their pretty heads, and how much they were destined, let us add, to put in them.

There was culture, and there were the arts as well, in the England that the Puritans put behind them. While it is quite true that many a one of the common folk, like Sampson, the servant in *Romeo and Juliet,* confronted with the written word, was compelled, scratching his head, to "resort to the learned"; there were still a-plenty who read and cared to read, who wrote and were able to write, and who loved and cultivated letters. Have you ever happened to look into a book, collected a few years since and entitled *A Short-Term Catalogue of Books Printed in England, Scotland and Ireland, and of English Books Printed Abroad up to 1640?* There are 609 pages of this book in double column, and 26,143 individual items. With a recollection of the hundreds of books that have perished, one could hardly call the Elizabethan an illiterate age. Indeed, scarcely a variety of book was wanting to the Elizabethan age, and many of them were so handsomely designed and artistically printed that when we want to produce a distinguished volume today we are most likely to succeed if we seek our model from among them. More, modern enumeration cannot name a kind of book as to content, from the ponderous tomes of divinity or solid histories, treatises on the arts of statecraft, navigation, geography, horsemanship, hunting, to essays, "characters," and dramas, from lengthy epics, pastoral verses, and dainty lyrics, to biting satires, lampoons, ballads, and broadsides—which did not issue in a continuous stream from the teeming presses of the day. The Elizabethans were great readers and greater lovers of plays and pageantry, in all of which they demanded a richness and profusion of ideas as well as a fitting and beautiful raiment, in all of which the spirit of artistry speaks forth in greater or lesser degree. I have often maintained the paradox that Shakespeare in his time, as ever since, was quite one of the best sellers. He did all he could to keep out of print in his day, because he was primarily interested in getting people to come and see his plays acted, not in having them stay at home to read them. But half of them got into print, none the less. And many a spurious production was printed either with the effrontery of his borrowed name, or at least with his initials on the title page; for the name of William Shakespeare in his own day, as well as ever since, was one to conjure with. Once more, when his works were collected, a first edition of a book, selling at the purchasing value today of fifty dollars, was exhausted in eight or nine years, with only three persons in ten able to read and write, and only one in ten financially able to buy any book of value. The potential audience of Shakespeare was tiny in comparison with, say, that of Mr. Walpole or Mr. Priestley or any of our own American best sellers, whose possible readers include the British Empire, our America, and the enormous number who have added English as the first foreign tongue to their own language. But considering the number of people in Shakespeare's England able to read books, able to buy books, and cultivated enough to enjoy his plays by means of the written word as well as by means of the spoken one, the frequency of the publication of his works will compare favorably with all the potential millions of the readers of the *Forsyte Saga,* let us say, or the dramas of Mr. Shaw or our Mr. O'Neill.

But not only was the amount and variety of Elizabethan reading extraordinary, considering the small comparative population of England: let us think, too, of its quality—the poetry of Sidney, Spenser, and Donne, the drama of Marlowe, Shakespeare, and Jonson, the philosophy of Bacon, to name no other, the divinity of Hooker, and the cadenced organ music of the incomparable prose of the King James version of our English Bible. This last, be it ever remembered, our Pilgrim fathers *put not behind them,* but bore it ever with them, the deep ground-tone of its music, when some of them ruthlessly banished the arts from their lives and worship, remaining the preservative of the sense of beauty in their rugged souls. Even when Shakespeare is left out of the count, Elizabethan poetry is the most expansive, the most spontaneous, the most artistically successful poetry that the English language has ever produced; and an age is always best judged in what it writes down deliberately for preservation in times to come. For if a nation's roads tell us how we go about in our day, how fast and how successfully we crawl from place to place upon the surface of the earth, how now our novel locomotion lifts us a little off that surface or plunges us a trifle beneath it, a nation's poetry, a nation's literature, even its mere balladry, tell the yearnings after the ideal, the flights of the imagination, the reachings out of the spirit into a region whither mechanism has not yet reached, nor, indeed, is ever to reach.

But the cunning of the word was not alone: this Elizabethan was the great age of English music, music as an art to be participated in, to be acquainted with and traversed in practice; not listened to in semi-ignorant appreciation and in wonder as to what it is all about, an art to which strange foreigners are addicted and for which Americans are generously willing to pay out good money, though one could hardly condescend to practise it. Some of the old Elizabethan music is delightful to listen to today, if you can continue to remain old-fashioned enough in spirit; and there is still joy in the part-song madrigals and motets, the airs and even the concerted compositions of Dr. Bull, Campion, Morley and many others. Indeed, the Elizabethans so esteemed music that they put it on a level of equality with poetry itself, as a pleasing and often-quoted sonnet, which you will find printed in the copy of your Shakespeare at home, proclaims. It runs:

> If music and sweet poetry agree,
> As they must needs, the sister and the brother,
> Then must the love be great 'twixt thee and me,
> Because thou lov'st the one and I the other.
> Dowland to thee is dear, whose heavenly touch
> Upon the lute doth ravish human sense;
> Spenser to me, whose deep conceit is such

As, passing all conceit, needs no defence.
Thou lov'st to hear the sweet melodious sound
That Phœbus' lute, the queen of music, makes;
And I in deep delight am chiefly drown'd
Whenas himself to singing he betakes.
One god is god of both, as poets feign;
One knight loves both, and both in thee remain.

This sonnet is not really by Shakespeare but by one Richard Barnefield, who admired the great dramatist so much that he tried to write lyrically like him and, in one or two happy instances, almost succeeded.

Have you ever had the good fortune to visit one of the great Tudor houses, Haddon Hall, Penshurst, seat of the Sidneys, Hatfield, or Burghley House at Stamford? In this last, as in many others, you traverse beautiful hall after hall, hung and decorated with the treasures of Italian and other art, furniture, tapestries, pictures, ornaments and what not; a Raphael or Michael Angelo, bought when Raphael or Michael Angelo was but a generation ago; a Titian, Holbein, or Tintoretto carried back by my Lord, Elizabeth's great earl of Burghley, on his return as a young man from the grand tour. And what, too, of the beauty of these Tudor and Stuart mansions themselves, their stately terraces and arcades, their grand and studied proportions, their graceful balanced towers and sweeping staircases, their sunlit walks, such as that in which Malvolio practised deportment, their parks and formal gardens, scene of many a masque and drama such as *Love's Labour's Lost?*

From a wider point of view, Elizabeth's was above all an age of great projects and of grandiose ideas. The splendid courtier Raleigh, locked up in the Tower, employed his enforced leisure with no less a theme than the history of the world; and, when he was temporarily released, wagered his life on the discovery of El Dorado up the Orinoco River—and lost the wager. Spenser planned a stupendous epic to rival the *Iliad* or the *Aeneid,* and died, only half of his great allegory on the ideal of true chivalry in man, *The Faerie Queene,* completed. Michael Drayton attempted and measurably succeeded in achieving an enormous topographical description of all England in verse, forgetting scarcely a hillock or a rivulet. And Hakluyt, year after year, collected every voyage into foreign parts that he could lay his hands on, translated, studied, gathered maps, published, and lectured to widen information as to the new world of commerce and adventure which was opening to the astonished comprehension of men. It was Hakluyt who foresaw the possibility, the glory of an English empire, rivaling that of haughty Spain in the new world, and courting comparison with that of imperial Rome. Francis Bacon, modestly taking "all human knowledge for his province," began with an inventory of all that had been done before him and dared the creation of a new process of reasoning, as he thought, with which to conquer an equally imperial empire among the sciences by means of the intellect of man. It was Bacon, too, who once more dreamed an ideal commonwealth in which, among other amazingly modern ideas, was to be realized much that we have scarcely yet reached in the way of laboratories for the advancement of human knowledge and the encouragement of scientific research.

With grandiose projects such as these went a proud certainty as to the power and future of the language which could thus sustain the wisdom of statesmen and divines and the flights of Elizabethan drama and poetry. An excellent old courtly poet named Samuel Daniel bursts forth thus, apostrophizing the potency of the English language to accomplish more

with one poor pen
Than all the powers of princes can effect;
And draw, divert, dispose, and fashion men
Better than force or rigor can direct.

And he asks, as to that glorious English tongue which is ours,

Should we this instrument of glory then
As th' unmaterial fruit of shades neglect?
Or should we careless come behind the rest
In power or words that go before in worth?

And then comes this remarkable prophecy, written, mind you, in the year 1599, when *Henry V*, *Hamlet*, and *As You Like It* were novelties on the stage, when the old queen was aging but still a power in the world:

And who in time knows whither we may vent
The treasure of our tongue, to what strange shores
This gain of our best glory shall be sent,
T'enrich unknowing nations with our stores?
What worlds in the yet unformèd occident
May 'come refined with th' accents that are ours?
Or who can tell for what great work in hand
The greatness of our style is now ordained,
What powers it shall bring in, what spirits command,
What thoughts let out, what humors keep restrained,
What mischief it may powerfully withstand,
And what fair ends may thereby be attained?

THE LAND THE PURITANS LEFT

The England that the Puritans put behind them was a gracious land. There was faith in it, for many besides the Puritans who left it believed in God, in the King, and in England. Some there were who suffered for the medieval faith of their forefathers with its sanction of the ages, its elaborate ritual, its sumptuous glorification of God. And others stopped with a faith that, preserving the past, yet repudiated interference by any other power in the affairs of the land of their birthright. And there was faith, in the old age, in station, in the sovereign as God-appointed, in men whose obligations of rank were as binding as the obligations of a bond. There were things, too, in England that could not be bought—let us remember this in our purchasable age—there was honor in men, courtesy to women, fidelity in servants, a nice sense of the obligations of rank, *noblesse oblige*—that subtle relation that we have to go to a foreign language to express. And there was faith, too, in beauty, in charming and artistic things, in noble buildings, in municipal pride, and a flourishing countryside, however the goddess Hygeia was served at few altars. If you doubt any of these things, read your Shakespeare, who mirrored his age, too honest to misrepresent it. Read your Spenser, who held up an enchanting ideal of that chivalry which is the soul of all veritable gentility. Read your Bacon, who, stumbling among the devious courses of a dishonest career, contrived, none the less, to see from afar the great time to come when man should avow his sovereignty in the conquest of inanimate matter and the yoking of nature to his service.

The land that the Puritans put behind them is gone; but it is something that our race once dwelt in such an age at home, however it may have gone out of it and beyond it. From the blaze and glare of today it is good sometimes to indulge in the twilight reverie of forgotten days, especially when that memory fires the imagination and sustains that hope without which we cannot go forward. The Elizabethan blood in our American veins is not the least noble of our heritages, and the Puritan courage which could deny all that glittered in that golden time to face hardship and despair for principle is not the least element in the American national strength which, let us pray, God may continue ever to be ours.

Memorial of Horace Howard Furness

It is a beautiful thought, that of Maeterlinck, that the consciousness, and therefore the mortality or immortality, of those who have gone before depends upon the recollection of the friends whom they have left behind them. In the dim netherworld sits many a one, like Saturn, quiet as a stone, unquickened because the image of him and of his doings has perished from the memory of the living. Others stir, as troubled in sleep, when the recollections of unkindness and ungentle deeds dart their twinges from the minds of those who still suffer in remembrance into the souls that have once done wrong. Only those really live whose pulses are quickened by that after-recognition of their achievements in the world which we call repute, and some even among these lie in enduring obloquy, execrated by generations of men, while fewer dwell, cold and aloof, in the silent halls of fame. Radiant and upright alone to walk with God is he whose memory smells sweet to heaven, exhaling from the hearts of all who knew him an image pure, beautiful, and serene. Let such be the image of our contemplation and our oblations; a simulacrum, alas, of the man that we knew, in whose memory we are met in befitting awe, reverence, and tenderness.

It is customary to speak of world-wide reputations and to dwell on superlatives when death has taken from among us one who has stood somewhat above his fellows. Here superlatives can barely reach the truth. The eminence of Dr. Furness in the scholarship of his chosen field was not merely that of survivorship. With names even such as those of Collier, of Halliwell-Phillipps, and Furnivall, our American scholar may well hold his own. Indeed, in generous recognition of all that English, German, and French scholarship has done the last fifty years—a recognition which Dr. Furness would have been the first graciously to concede—it may be confidently affirmed that in the death of the editor of the *New Variorum Shakespeare* the world suffered the loss of the most notable authority on the plays of Shakespeare of our time. And his work was *sui generis,* involving not only an acquaintance with the text, the style, the thought, the outlook on life and art of the great dramatist, but that more difficult knowledge to acquire with patience and use with discretion, the collected mass of criticism, opinion, conjecture, theory, and surmise of Shakespeare commentary.

Dr. Furness, as is well known, came of literary stock. His father, Dr. William Henry Furness, was a writer of distinction, a personal friend of Emerson, and a leader among the Abolitionists, as among the Unitarians whose ministry he graced. Transplanted from his native New England, he lived a great part of his life in Philadelphia, radiating the influence of an unaffected piety and spirituality of ideals that made for unmixed good. The sister, too, of Dr. Horace Howard Furness, the late Mrs. Casper Wister, so dear to the many who knew her, enjoyed a deserved literary reputation as a translator. Nor did the children of Dr. Furness fail to carry on the family tradition.

Horace Howard Furness the elder was born in Philadelphia, November 2, 1833, and after receiving his preparatory training there, entered Harvard, graduating with the class of 1854. He subsequently studied law, and would have practised his profession but for the early development of deafness, which subsequently defeated also his desire to serve his country actively on the field in the time of the Civil War. The years 1855 and 1856 Dr. Furness spent in foreign travel, and in 1859 he married Miss Helen Kate Rogers, of Philadelphia. Circumstances may be said to have conspired to make Dr. Furness a scholar, his infirmity cutting him off from an active career, sufficient means making it possible for him to go through the necessary period of preparation and to await the gradual approach of that slow success which is likely, in pure scholarship at least, to prove most lasting. It has been remarked that Dr. Furness was one of the last of that fortunate type of scholar who, in place of going out to seek his material, gathered it about him and made his own library his workshop. Like his friend and fellow townsman, the late Henry C. Lea, in a very different field, Dr. Furness was a collector, and to need a book was to add it, at some time sooner or later, to his collection. But, unlike our contemporary book-hunter who collects volumes as one might gather together curiosities to hoard them in strongholds, Dr. Furness' collections had ever the scholar's purpose, and the result is a library of Shakespeare texts and commentary, exhibiting not a few rarities, but valuable above all to the legitimate purposes for which it was created. It may not be impertinent here to interpolate, that this practicable and useful library is now the property of the University of Pennsylvania, the gracious and generous gift by bequest of the late Horace Howard Furness, Jr., and Louise Windsor Furness, his wife. It has, in accordance with the plan and request of the donors, been handsomely and appropriately housed in a charming room, modeled after the Library of Merton College, Oxford, and funds are available (also by the considerate terms of the bequest) for the maintenance of a custodian and the purchase of books, further to increase the richness and volume of the collection.

The interest of Dr. Furness in Shakespeare began in his boyhood, before he went to college; and it was cherished by the remarkable readings of the plays by the notable actress and author, Frances Anne Kemble. As the daughter of Charles Kemble and the niece of the famous Mrs. Siddons, Fanny Kemble brought to her readings of Shakespeare some of the finest traditions of the English stage, handed down, many of them in unwritten customs, from the earlier days of Garrick and Betterton. This, added to a rich and resonant voice, a fine presence and a knowledge and experience derived from actual contact with the stage, gave to her readings a quality which might well captivate and entrance one already an ardent lover of Shakespeare. With the open sesame of the reader's card on which was written the magic words, "Admit Mr. Furness to all my readings," the young student of Shakespeare "never missed one," and thus formed at once the foundation of his own sound scholarship and remarkable quality as a reader of Shakespeare.

In the Shakspere Society of Philadelphia, too, the young enthusiast found a group of men congenial to his tastes; and to this society he later dedicated the first volume of his work. The Shakspere Society had been founded years before by a coterie of young men, lovers of Shakespeare and students of the plays. But foremost among those who encouraged the young editor in his undertaking with sympathy, counsel, and suggestions, the fruit of his own rich and various learning, was George Allen, Professor of Greek in the University of Pennsylvania, who read the proofs of the two or three earlier volumes of the *New Variorum* and set for the work, once and for all, the ideal of precise and exact scholarship.

The idea of editing *A New Variorum Edition of Shakespeare* was a gradual growth in the projector's mind. As early as 1850, Dr. Furness' interest in the tragedy of *Hamlet* had induced him to read the earlier commentators on that play and to make up for his own use a copy of *Hamlet* in which he incorporated not only the earlier notes collected by Malone and Boswell in what is known as the *Third*

Variorum Edition of 1821, but likewise as much comment, the work of later editors, as was accessible to him at that time. Dr. Furness had long been sensible of the fact that it was only upon the foundation of what had preceded him that any editor of Shakespeare could hope to build any new fabric of his own; and, with a recognition of the amount and value of what had gone before, there gradually arose in him a determination to perform the great and needed service of the editor of a variorum Shakespeare, and to perform this service thoroughly and completely. Some years passed after this determination was formed, years of study and devotion, and with the mistrust which is born of knowledge, Dr. Furness chose as his first volume, not *Hamlet,* but *Romeo and Juliet,* a choice, on his own confession, made from a sheer love of the glorious poetry of that most passionate of the dramas of love.

The first volume of *A New Variorum Edition of Shakespeare* appeared in 1871. The need of such a work was apparent in contemplation of the great mass and valuable content of the comment on Shakespeare which had accumulated since the days of Malone, its inaccessibility to the average student, scattered as it was in hundreds of volumes and pamphlets, in various tongues, unedited and unindexed. With a due acknowledgment of the critical and textual value of the *Cambridge Shakespeare* of 1863, which had given "a thorough and minute collation of the quartos and folios and a majority of the *variae lectiones* of many modern editors, together with many conjectural emendations," Dr. Furness thus set forth his own plan. This included first, "a complete collation of the four folios, four out of the five quartos of *Romeo and Juliet,* and the texts of thirty-five editions," and secondly, the collection and abridgment, "after the manner of a variorum," of all the comments and emendations of critics of this play, "and the presenting of them, on the same page, in a condensed form, in connection with the difficulties which they explain." In the text of this first volume the editor followed, "as a general rule . . . the reading of the majority of the ablest editors, but not always." This rule, which involved the making of an independent text, was adhered to in the earlier volumes. With the appearance of *King Lear,* in 1880, Dr. Furness reverted to the text of the first folio, and to that text he adhered ever after. "Be it," he writes, "that the pages of this first folio are little better than proof-sheets, lacking the supervision of the author or of any other, yet 'those who had Shakespeare's manuscript before them were more likely to read it right than we who read it only in imagination,' as Dr. Johnson said." Since these words were written, Shakespeare criticism has turned ever more and more to a recognition of the essential integrity of the old versions, until with the recent triumph of Mr. Pollard's bibliographical optimism applied both to quartos and folios over the grudging pessimism of many a notable predecessor, Dr. Furness' opinion of thirty years ago assumes the guise of prophecy.

The *New Variorum Shakespeare* included, as Dr. Furness left it, fourteen plays; and on one more, *Cymbeline,* his work was practically complete at the time of his death. This has long since appeared. Only those who have dipped into the strong current of Shakespeare criticism, with its dangerous hidden rocks and its undertow that means annihilation, can conceive of the strength of thew, the steadiness of head, and the soundness of heart that alone can sustain the hardy swimmer in these troubled waters. Dr. Furness displayed a great dexterity in the avoidance of prolixity and repetition among the commentators, and he diligently sifted the huge rubbish heaps of unintelligent Shakespeare criticism for the pearls that have occasionally been lost therein. But it cannot be said that he misrepresented in any particular the huge fabric of Shakespeare comment, which is, in many respects, the most surprising, fertile, interesting, and at times subtle and invaluable structure which men have reared to the perpetuation of their mingled wisdom and folly.

Dr. Furness' work is technically the fourth variorum. An edition of Shakespeare furnished "with select notes from all the commentators" was projected by Edmund Malone as early as 1783. The first edition of Malone's Shakespeare appeared in 1790; but it was not in any real sense a variorum edition, and it is never so called. "The 'first variorum' is the name bestowed on the edition of Johnson and Steevens, edited by Isaac Reed in 1803; and the 'second variorum' is that bestowed on the revision of Isaac Reed's work, issued in 1813." The revision of Malone's second edition by James Boswell, a son of the biographer of Dr. Johnson, is the "third variorum," which is thus the final outcome of Malone's original plan of 1783. This excellent work appeared in 1821 in twenty-two volumes, under the title: *The Plays and Poems of William Shakespeare, with corrections and illustrations of various commentators: comprehending a life of the poet and an enlarged history of the stage.* Boswell takes a very modest share of this work to himself, and strikes the note of a variorum editor in the remark, "According to the plan laid down by Mr. Malone, I have inserted all the notes of his predecessors, although I am ready to admit that some of them might well have been spared. And again here I request it may be understood that my passing them over in silence is not to be considered as acquiescing in their propriety." The prolegomena of Boswell's edition contain reprints of the prefaces, introduction, and "proposals" of the previous editions of Shakespeare from Rowe, Pope, and Theobald to Steevens and Reed, with a general gathering of material bearing on the life and times of Shakespeare, the contemporary drama, and contributory forms of literature, criticism and other matter. The variorum feature exhibits the various readings and emendations of the text in footnotes on the same page, ascribing each to its editor.

From the year 1783, in which Malone first conceived his plan, to 1821, thirty-eight years had elapsed, and this had sufficed to complete a work which adequately represented the then fabric of Shakespeare criticism in its mass and in its detail. With the fifty years which had passed between the "third variorum" and the appearance of the first volume of Dr. Furness' *New Variorum,* the material to be included had much more than doubled. In England Shakespeare comment had taken a new and highly important departure in the æsthetic criticism of Coleridge; and that fine, instinctive sympathy with the inner springs and niceties of poetic thought and expression which defies analysis and takes to itself wings where other criticism painfully measures its way and crawls, had found its choicest exponent in lovable Charles Lamb. Malone had England alone to reckon with; by the time that Dr. Furness came to his task not only had America contributed her respectable quota of comment written in Shakespeare's own tongue, but critics writing in foreign tongues had swelled the chorus of Shakespeare praise and explanation to an orchestral tumult in which were many new, significant, and insistent notes. One of the most lasting fruits of Voltaire's visit to England, as far back as 1726, had been a somewhat casual acquaintance with the plays of Shakespeare. And although Voltaire changed from enthusiastic admiration to scorn and all but contempt for his "discovery," appreciation for the English poet by the few continued in France until, with the rise of the romantic school of Victor Hugo, kinship of spirit has given to the great romantic dramatist an ever wider vogue in France. But it was long after the appearance of the "third variorum" before Frenchmen began to apply to the study of Shakespeare that finely tempered literary acumen which distinguishes the criticism of their tongue. Now we must take into account many eminent Shakespeare scholars in France; not least among them the late distinguished ambassador of that fraternal country to our own, M. Jusserand, who united with us on this memorial occasion to honor the memory of the American scholar. Much later than Voltaire, that admirable critic, Lessing, discovered Shakespeare for Germany and revealed the dramatist to his countrymen, though not to the English-speaking world, as the prideful German is even yet at times fond of boasting. How would Dr. Johnson have scouted the idea that a time should one day come in which no critic of Shakespeare could be considered adequately equipped who was not prepared to reckon with the French and dispute it with the Germans! And yet such is actually the case. The intellectual activity of Germany in this as in all subjects—be it said to her immortal credit—has continued in an ever increasing ratio, until not to know the language of the Fatherland has long been considered as hopeless a bar to sound and thorough scholarship in Shakespeare as in anything else.

With all this in view, it was a daring thing for a man scarcely more than thirty, measurably removed from the literary treasure houses of the world (which means so much in an undertaking of this kind), to conceive of a plan so stupendous; and the restraint and unselfish fidelity to high ideals with which the work has been carried out is even more surprising. The temptation to press on to completion must, to some natures, have proved irresistible. The allurements which beset the editor in the prosecution of such a work are legion. How fond men are of the expression of an opinion or of the turning of a quibble when Shakespeare is in question, these volumes of the *Variorum Shakespeare* abundantly attest. But through all, the sage yet kindly judge preserves the fine decorum of a court of equity, suffering the tedious man to be heard and the fool to convict himself in his folly. Dr. Furness recognized no aristocracy in criticism, and allowed neither the tongue nor the temper of those whom he cited to interfere with their testimony or to ruffle his own patient and courteous hearing. As he put it himself: "Those who read and study these volumes may be safely trusted to discover for themselves the wisdom or folly of the critics, and the editor gladly foregoes the pleasure of displaying how much wiser he is than those whom he cites." For the decision of each case we have words sufficient and no more; and only too rare are the occasions in which the judge is betrayed into those choice *obiter dicta* which, while they may determine no immediate issue, have often a significance of wider and weightier import.

However, no one who reads the delightful prefaces and appendices to the volumes of the *Variorum Shakespeare* need remain in doubt as to the attitude of the editor in essential matters of Shakespeare criticism. For example, Dr. Furness deals with the much-mooted questions involved in a consideration of the chronology of certain plays, in all their vexatious details and with honest and painstaking fidelity, but he also displays his own attitude towards such questions: "Could we be content with dry, prosaic facts," he says, "this discussion in the present play would be brief. Meres mentions *A Midsummer-Night's Dream,* among others, in 1598. This is all we know. But in a discussion over any subject connected with Shakespeare, who ever heard of resting content with what we know? It is what we do not know that fills our volumes." And again: "Would it add a charm to Portia's quality of mercy if we knew that it was written in 1594—in August—on the fifth day—on Wednesday—in the afternoon—at twenty minutes past three o'clock? Is it any tribute to Shakespeare's genius that we should busy ourselves over what is not even in the setting of the gem, but no more than the jeweler's case in which it is sent home?" Of the varying moods in which we read the plays we find the following:

Hours there are, and they come to us all, when we want no voice, charm it never so wisely, to break in upon Shakespeare's own words. If there be obscurity, we rather like it; if the meaning be veiled, we prefer it veiled. Let the words flow on in their own sweet cadence, lulling our sense, charming our ears, and let all sharp quillets cease. When Amiens' gentle voice sings of the winter wind that its tooth is not so keen because it is not seen, who of us ever dreams, until wearisome commentators gather mumbling around that there is in the line the faintest flaw in logical sequence? But this idle, receptive mood does not last forever. The time comes when we would fain catch every ray of light flashing from these immortal plays, and pluck the heart out of every mystery there; then, then, we listen respectfully and gratefully to every suggestion, every passing thought which obscure passages have stirred and awakened in minds far finer than our own.

The *Variorum Shakespeare* was not long in receiving the recognition which was its due, although Dr. Furness used to delight in telling the story of its refusal by cautious publishers and how he had undertaken the whole venture from the first at his own risk. As far back as 1877, his own alma mater, Harvard, recognized the undertaking with an honorary degree, and later the University of Pennsylvania, Columbia, and Harvard once more, honored themselves in thus honoring him. Abroad Dr. Furness received an honorary degree from the

University of Halle and was made president of the German Shakespeare Society. He was among the earliest members of the American Institute and Academy of Arts and Letters, to say nothing of other learned societies. Finally, in 1899, he received the degree of Doctor of Letters from the University of Cambridge, England.

Among many activities, none of which were allowed to interfere with his great task, Dr. Furness gave years of service to the counsels of the Board of Trustees of the University of Pennsylvania, occupying himself especially in the needs of the library, wherein his solicitude and advice bore fortunate fruit. Too rare a speaker yet peculiarly happy in substance and charm of manner, whatever his subject, it was always an event in Philadelphia when Dr. Furness could be induced to read Shakespeare. This he did latterly only on rare occasions, for charity or for the favored few whose happy fortune it was to be near him. Almost the last semi-public reading of Dr. Furness was at the annual dinner of the Shakspere Society of Philadelphia, when he read to less than a score of us one of his favorite plays, *The Winter's Tale*. Those who were present will remember that he seemed never in better voice, never in happier vein than when he read and at times half chanted in a beautiful art now lost to us who remain, the rollicking songs of Autolycus. Yet there was ever about Dr. Furness in these latter years an undertone of sadness. His bereavements had been many, and while he suffered them never to interfere with the cheerfulness of those about him, to which his ready wit, his prodigious memory, and happy agility of thought constantly contributed, it was plain to those who knew him best that sorrow had left its mark upon him.

Horace Howard Furness was an old-fashioned scholar and an old-fashioned man. He recalled at all times that leisure is an essential of sound scholarship, not leisure to dawdle, but leisure to do what is to be done wholly and completely no matter what the time involved; leisure to read, to know, to be infinitely more than the narrow specialist, digging one ditch in oblivion of the world about and the skies above. His was the old-fashioned courtesy that has time to remember trifles and to be kind to unconsidered persons. His generosity to young scholars was abounding. Time and again did he spread the treasures of his library and the more precious treasures of his time for their faltering acceptance; and his modesty alone exceeded his bounty. I never saw him angry save where some act of oppression or ungenerosity was in question, and then his indignation knew no bounds. For the arrogance of petty scholarship he had an amused smile; for even small, if genuine accomplishment, an ungrudging and instant recognition. That charming, galleried room at Wallingford, with its profusion of pictures, relics, and mementos, most of them touching Shakespeare—who that had once seen it can ever forget? And the books, from the latest doctor's thesis, German, French, English, or American, with the paper-knife inserted between its leaves, as yet half-cut, to the stately folios of Shakespeare (as I remember, at least some seven copies in number) and the even choicer quartos, acquired by a scholar for a scholar's use, and shrined with other treasures in a sacred seclusion. To have met the white-haired genius of the place, his smile of welcome, his unaffected courtesy; the story that rose to his lips in reminiscence, the anecdote suggested by the ancient book in hand or by the mention of some old actor, the grasp of friendship's hand at parting—these were brave sublunary things to live while memory lasts. As I turn over the precious letters that Dr. Furness on various occasions wrote me—alas, only too few, and depleted with losses—I find, as other friends have found, not one on which is not stamped, with a touch too subtle for analysis, that indefinable charm that was his. I had written—more often I went—for advice as to a point on that somewhat wooden hobby, the construction of the old English stage. About this subject, it may be remarked, in the old phrase, there had been "much knocking about of brains." "Don't ask me," he replied, "about the staging of Elizabethan plays. The only conclusion I can draw from the whole discussion is that they never were staged at all." Within the last year of his life he writes:

Do you not know that in this worky-day world few things can be more welcome than *laudari a laudato?* In looking on what I have accomplished, it seems as though I had only nibbled at the circumference. . . . My race is run and it is for me to wish you long years of happy work.

In the words of excellent old Michael Drayton, Shakespeare's intimate, whose works Dr. Furness loved and approved:

He was a man (then boldly dare to say)
  In whose rich soul the virtues well did suit,
In whom so mixed the elements all lay
  That none to one could sovereignty impute,
As all did govern yet all did obey;
  He of temper was so absolute
As that it seemed when nature him began
She meant to show all that might be in man.

Shakespeare Books in the Library of the Furness Memorial

I HAVE been asked to describe some of the treasures contained in the Library of the Furness Memorial, and I find the promise to do so far easier than the fulfillment—this for at least two reasons, first, the multiplicity and variety of the items in such a collection and, secondly, a personal limitation that leaves me cold in the contemplation of what may be called the trappings and insignia of greatness. The world is dotted with mausoleums and museums harboring the relics —better the old word "remains"—of heroes, from the saddle or equine throne of the victor of Agincourt, placed high on a beam in Westminster Abbey, to a replica in wax—if report is to be trusted—of the last meal refused by an otherwise indistinguishable youth who gave his name to the foundation of a large American institution of learning. The Furness Memorial contains a number of mementos: pieces of wood, some expertly fashioned, from the old mulberry tree which tradition relates that Shakespeare planted with his own hand in 1609, later chopped down by an irate parson because it attracted too many pilgrims to his garden; a splinter of the oaken beam from the room in which the great poet was born; most treasured, a pair of gloves which tradition as far back as Betterton relates were once veritably Shakespeare's. Another kind of interest attaches to the walking stick, deeply carved with the name of Rosalind, which Mr. Otis Skinner once carried when acting Orlando with the celebrated Madame Modjeska; to the set of recorders or flageolets, fingered by Booth in *Hamlet* and declared in the handling "as easy as lying"; the dirk of Macbeth worn by the same great actor; Sir Henry Irving's Shylock's cloak and Hamlet's black shirt; and, last, not least, a skull, inscribed with the names of Keene, Macready, Kemble, and our own Forrest and Booth, which had been tossed out on the stage time out of mind and handled and ruminated upon, abundantly justifying the phrase of the text: "Alas, poor Yorick, I knew him well." My limitation has betrayed me into flippancy, for which, grave reader, be merciful. For those who care for such relics, there are several things worth serious mention in this collection. I must leave to others more sympathetic than I the appreciation which very properly dignifies the collector of them and those who can imaginatively reconstruct the past out of these pathetic remnants of time.

Let us turn to the books which have an entity even apart from association. To begin with the repetition of some of the commonplaces, the famous First Folio, earliest collective edition of Shakespeare's plays, appeared in 1623, seven years after the poet's death. It contained not only a reprint of all, except one, of the plays which had previously appeared in separate quarto editions (seventeen in number), but about as many more which, protected by the King's company who owned the manuscripts, had not previously appeared in print. Naturally this famous book must form the foundation stone of any Shakespeare library; for as to nearly half the plays it is the *editio princeps;* and as to the rest, no matter what the quartos, the Folio is never negligible. The Furness collection contains a good example of this much-sought-for volume, which is recorded in Lee's Census of Extant Copies as having been "well used; fly-leaf, letterpress of title and last page [however as frequently] made up in facsimile by Harris; the inserted portrait . . . from an original copy." Lee further records that this volume once belonged to Thomas Corser, the well-known editor of *Collectanea Anglo-Poetica,* who acquired his love of Elizabethan literature while at Oxford, in the first decade of the nineteenth century, through intimacy with Dr. Henry Cotton, sub-librarian of the Bodleian, and early became an indefatigable collector of earlier English books. Only one purchaser intervened between Corser and Dr. Furness. This stately volume, in its honestly worn red and gold, declares a long and sturdy aid to scholarship. There could have been none better used among its brethren. The First Folio, despite the eagerness with which it is sought and the notably rising prices which copies of it appear steadily to maintain with the judicious aid of booksellers, is by no means what the bibliophiles would call a rare volume. No less than 156 copies were listed in various states of completeness as far back as 1902, and something near to two hundred are now known to exist.[1] Most interesting is it to note that such a survival even of tatterdemalions—until their rags were doffed and they were rearrayed as princes—points to two things at least: an original edition not inconsiderable in size—caution forbids the mention of numbers; [2] and a popularity which bought up and used this book to its partial destruction. It is the unread book that stands in pristine integrity neglected on the shelves. Popular books are literally read to pieces.

This *editio princeps* of the collected works of Shakespeare was followed by a second folio in 1632, a third in 1663–64, and a fourth in 1685. Obviously, however, these later editions are less interesting and therefore less valuable, though none is safely to be neglected in questions of text involving differences and possible corrections. The notion

[1] Sidney Lee, *Shakespeare's Comedies . . . a Census,* 1902, p. 33; and *The Folger Shakespeare Library,* 1933, p. 17, where we learn this library has seventy-nine copies.

[2] See W. W. Greg, *The Bibliographical History of the First Folio,* N. S., IV, 1903, p. 265.

that, in relation to the First Folio and the quartos, these later folios only make a bad matter worse, has long since gone into the discard with other assumptions based on a partial knowledge.[3] The Furness collection contains good copies of each of the second and third folios, and two of the fourth. An interesting feature of the third folio, as is well known, is the admission into it of seven additional plays not printed in the First Folio. Save for *Pericles,* which had already appeared in several quartos previously, none of these additions is now accepted as work of Shakespeare, although a library pro and con on the topic has long since sprung up and faded, to wither on forgotten bookshelves.[4]

The quartos, or single plays, whether printed in the author's lifetime and before the appearance of the First Folio or later, form the second group in a Shakespeare library. Those subsequent to the First Folio are textually of minor value; those before its appearance, never to be neglected. For while it is undoubtedly true that some of these little books of single plays were "stolen and surreptitious copies," we are coming more and more to appreciate the significance of the quartos of Shakespeare which appeared before the date of the poet's death, for it is obvious that there is something to be said for the text of a book which the author might possibly have seen as contrasted with one which he could never have set eyes on; though each case of the Folio *versus* the quartos is to be judged independently and upon its own merits.

[3] See a forthcoming study of *Shakespeare's Seventeenth Century Editors,* by Black and Shaaber, and the earlier authoritative work of A. W. Pollard, *Shakespearean Folios and Quartos,* 1904.

[4] See P. Simpson, *Proof-Reading in the Sixteenth, Seventeenth and Eighteenth Centuries,* 1935, especially, and the earlier researches of Pollard, McKerrow, Greg and many others.

Of the seventeen plays of Shakespeare which appeared in separate or quarto forms before the date of the First Folio, some forty-five separate editions all told, the Furness Library possesses only a few, none of them first editions. Quartos of such quality described in their rarity as literally worth their weight not in gold but in "banknotes and those notes by no means for the smallest sums," [5] have long since passed beyond the reach of mere scholarship; to be returned to scholarship's uses, however, by that fine sense of responsibility, of ultimate justice, that has prompted such magnificent foundations as those of the late Henry C. Folger and Henry E. Huntington. For example, there are no two more priceless volumes in all Shakespeareana than the first quarto of *Hamlet,* 1603, two imperfect copies of which alone are extant—one in the British Museum, the other in the Huntington Library at San Marino, California; [6] and the absolutely unique quarto of *Titus Andronicus,* earliest play attaching to the name of Shakespeare, now in the Folger Shakespeare Library in Washington. Reproduction of such treasures by our modern means of photostat returns them happily to the uses of scholarship.

To return to the Furness books, this collection possesses twenty-three quartos according to *A Census of Shakespeare's Plays in Quarto printed between 1594 and 1709,* prepared some years since.[7] There are really a few more. They vary in their states of preservation, completeness, and importance: all are of value, some of unusual interest. Somewhat to enumerate, there is a good copy of the third quarto of *Hamlet,* 1611, the earliest of the eight quartos of this master play in the collection. One of these, undated though possibly of 1630, ex-

[5] *A Census of Shakespeare's Plays in Quarto,* 1916. Introduction, p. ix.

[6] Now admirably reprinted in facsimile by the Huntington Library, 1931.

[7] By H. C. Bartlett and A. W. Pollard, 1916. According to the table on p. x of this work the sum total of first-edition quartos is only 146, two of them fragmentary.

hibits on the title-page an imitation of Shakespeare's signature. And it has been identified as one of the many fabricated by the impudent forger W. H. Ireland who, learning when a boy, listening to literary chatter in one of the later decades of the eighteenth century, that the authentic signatures of the great poet were exceedingly few, resolved that such a state of affairs needed remedy. Ireland's forgeries reached to the perpetration of whole plays: but happily they do not concern us. Other valuable quartos of the Furness collection are the Roberts' *Merchant of Venice,* 1600; a *Henry V* and a *King Lear* of 1608. All of these may be designated as second quartos. The two latter are further interesting in that the *Henry V* is one of several of these volumes presented to Dr. Furness as gifts of friendship by the famous Shakespearean J. O. Halliwell-Phillipps, author of the popular *Outlines of Shakespeare.* Others so presented and inscribed are *The Taming of the Shrew,* 1631, *The Merchant of Venice,* 1637, *King Lear,* 1655, an imperfect copy of the *Pericles* of 1619, and a fragment of the 1612 quarto of *Richard III.* The earlier *Lear,* 1608, mentioned above, contains manuscript notes by Edward Capell, an earlier distinguished editor of Shakespeare, but they are unimportant. Finally the collection includes, besides that mentioned above, another quarto of *Pericles,* 1630, and the 1631 edition of *Love's Labour's Lost,* to be designated a second or a third quarto as we reject or accept the theory of a lost first quarto prior to that of 1598. This item is not mentioned in the *Census.* It appears by an inscription to have been "presented to the Shakspere Society of Philadelphia, March 1870, by J. O. Halliwell," who had not at that time added "Phillipps" to his name. How it was returned to the Furness collection we are not informed.

Contemporary Elizabethan books in which there is mention or allusion to Shakespeare form a class eagerly sought for by collectors, and one well represented in this collection. However much we may have seen the quotation in schoolbooks, it is somewhat moving to read, in the swinging balance of Meres' "comparative discourse," *Wits Commonwealth* (first edition, 1598), how "Shakespeare among the English is most excellent in both kinds for the stage," and to continue through the familiar list of twelve of his plays, already popular at that early date and here printed together for the first time. It is this celebrated passage of contemporary evidence—enough for any court, if insufficient for Baconian or Oxfordian lack-logic—which has been declared by careful skepticism, "our only solid rock in a sea of surmise." But there are other rocks and footholds: witness the grudging jealousy of Greene's *Groatsworth of Wit,* 1592, Chettle's apology of the next year, Weever's epigram to "honie-tong'd Shakespeare," 1593, and the scores of others culled for us in the now overgrown *Shakespeare Allusion Book.*[8] The allusions just named do not exist in this library in their earliest forms; but there are a-plenty that do: Stowe's *Annales,* the second edition of which contains an enumeration of "our moderne and present excellent poets . . . orderly set down" and among them "Mr. Willi. Shakespeare gentleman": pray, note "gentleman"; similar lists in Heywood's *Rape of Lucrece* and Camden's *Remains,* 1614; Webster's words as to "the right happy and copious industry of Master Shakespeare"—note the "Master" (*Vittoria Corombona,* 1612); and the delightful passage of Heywood's *Hierarchie of the Blessed Angels,* 1635, in which, in a muster of good fellowship among the playwrights, each is familiarly docked as to his Christian name, and we read, to quote only a fragment:

> Excellent Bewmont, in the foremost ranke
> Of the rar'st Wits, was never more than Frank.

[8] Latest edition that of Sir Edmund Chambers, 2 vols., 1932.

Mellifluous Shakespeare, whose enchanting quill
Commanded mirth and passion, was but Will.
And famous Jonson, though his learned Pen
Be dipt in Castaly, is but Ben.

Leaving much else, we may read in Kirkman's *The Wits,* 1672, versions of Shakespeare's and other dramatists' comedies made into "drolls," as they were called—about as well as we might dare to do such scenes over into movies—this to escape Puritan penalties in a godly age that consorted ill with such frivolities as stage plays. Has even Mr. Masefield done much better with *Romeo and Juliet* for the screen? Best among these allusive books I like the fragment of John Wilson's *Cheerful Ayres,* 1660, which contains the music which Richard Johnson wrote contemporaneously for "Full fathom five thy father lies," Ariel's song in *The Tempest.* Now, if you will look into any copy of *Much Ado About Nothing* which has not been sophisticated by modern editing, you will find that (in II, iii) one Jack Wilson enters in the train of the Prince, but that the character, Balthasar (omitted from those entering), bandies words and excuses as singers do, and is prevailed upon at last to sing "Sigh no more, ladies." Wilson is no uncommon name. But is it not pleasurable to believe that young Jack Wilson, singing "Sigh no more, ladies" on the stage in 1599, may have ripened into Dr. John Wilson of Oxford, years later, to collect choice songs out of his memories of the past and include among them the later Shakespeare air, "Full fathom five"? Shall faith and confessions of faith have no more place in scholarship?

We come closer to Shakespeare in the works from which there is reason to believe that he derived his materials. Sources, I do not like to call them; for the mastery of genius does not borrow, but assumes his own wherever he may find it. The Furness collection contains admirable specimens of three of the four cornerstones of Shakespeare's personal library: Holinshed's *Chronicles* (first edition, 1574), for English history; North's translation of Plutarch (the edition of 1612), for the great men and deeds of the ancient world; Painter's *Palace of Pleasure* (originally 1575, in this collection only a much later edition), for much of his Italian story; and several fine copies of earlier English Bibles: for Shakespeare, the most untheological of the men of any age, was steeped in Scriptures. There is also Golding's *Metamorphoses* of Ovid, 1567, a fine classic spoiled in a clumsy translation: though sensible people no longer question Shakespeare's working competency in the Latin tongue. And there is Florio's *Montaigne* (in a later edition), of which the honest old counselor Gonzalo was certainly a reader; Munday's translation of Silvayn's *Orator,* 1596, which tells (as the French original had told far earlier) "of a Jew, who would for his debt have a pound of the flesh of a Christian," and the contemporary collections of Belforest, Bandello, and Cinthio in their original French and Italian; as to which there are those who conceive that Shakespeare may have been clouded in no such invincible ignorance as not to have been able to use them. Interesting it is to look into *The Royal Grammar,* "compiled formerly by Mr. William Lilly . . . now modestly endeavored to be rendered plain and obvious to the capacity of youth." Dr. Lilly was the grandfather of Shakespeare's earlier competitor in the drama, John Lyly. Shakespeare could have studied no other grammar (and grammar was only Latin) if he went to the Stratford Grammar School. Equally well known to him must have been Thomas Wilson's *The Arte of Rhetoricke,* 1584, from the fertile pages of which it has been thought that Shakespeare derived, among other things, suggestions for the funeral oration of Antony over Caesar's body, the character of Falstaff, and certain petty tricks in punctuation by which a letter may be made to read in divers ways. But enough—there is no end to "the sources of Shakespeare," whether he is conceived of as the least original of petty borrowers or as one who well may have said, with his own Pistol:

The world's mine oyster!

We have traversed some distance to reach only the fringe of that tangled and thorny jungle in which cavort the critical editors of Shakespeare. Let us pause before it is too late. The strangest book in any Shakespeare library is one entitled *Select Observations on English Bodies of Eminent Persons in Desperate Diseases,* 1679, by Mr. John Hall, Physician. Hall was Shakespeare's son-in-law and ran true to his calling, immersed in his "cures historical and empirical." Among his patients were many of the nobility or gentry of Warwickshire. We learn of "Mr. Drayton, an excellent poet, laboring of a tertian"; and that to his own wife, Elizabeth Hall, the doctor administered, among other medicaments and in the resulting cure most successfully, "a pint of sack made hot." This was Falstaff's favorite potation, be it remembered, but in no such ladylike proportions. We do not know that Hall ever ministered to the bodily needs of his august father-in-law. But we do know that we would give all his "wormwood, rue and fetherfew," his possets, "gellies of hartshorn with marygold flowers," his "sena cleansed and salt of Tatar" for a paragraph of what he thought of the man whose brain eternized Hamlet, Falstaff, and Cleopatra.

S. Weir Mitchell, Poet and Novelist

AMONG the customs of men sanctioned by time, there is none more honorable than the commemoration of those who have stood conspicuous among their fellows, earning by deed, conduct, and character the admiration and the homage of men. The leader, recognized as such, the man of power, he whom we can trust, to whom we turn at need, and who fails us never—such constitute alone that veritable nobility to which is reducible in time all our human pomp and pageantry, all our dignities and insignia. To be coveted above all treasure is it to have accomplished some one thing so completely, so indubitably as to earn the approval, the acclaim of those who know: to have left the world wiser, better, happier for having lived and labored in it. Nor is the commemoration of great names merely an act of justice. The understanding and recognition of worth, the tribute paid to superlative achievement, these are things that have in them the essence of piety; and bereft of the spirit of worship, man is scarcely man. It is therefore in accord with this most amply sanctioned of human institutions that we are met to honor the memory of Silas Weir Mitchell, physician of a fame world-wide, author in the forefront of those who have written delectable fiction in our English language, poet of a rare and acknowledged excellence. And Dr. Mitchell could not have achieved distinction in all of these memorable fields nor that recognition that transcends both time and place, had he not been as well a humane and kindly man, a faithful friend, a delightful host, a fine gentleman in the inimitable poise and dignity that belonged to a time more stately but not less human than our own; in a word, S. Weir Mitchell could not have been the eminently distinguished physician, novelist, and poet that he was had he not been as well both socially and civically, as professionally, the first Philadelphian of his day.

In this specialized, this differentiated age of ours, with each man cultivating his own little garden patch, oblivious of the tulips grown next door or the cabbages across the way, it is difficult to grasp the significance of a man so versatile, so curious as to everything, so keen in his vision alike as to what is near or far, a man so fruitfully thoughtful, ingenious, suggestive, and foreseeing as was Dr. Mitchell. We cannot even commemorate understandingly the many spheres in which he reached distinction except by means of coöperation: for it demands stature to measure greatness; and the medical and scientific expert, in I know not how many fields, must combine with the critic, the historian, the appraiser of fiction and the appreciator of poetry, if we are, in united effort, to estimate the multiple activities of this remarkable man. Even with his eminent contributions to science and his leadership in his profession left out, I cannot but feel the magnitude of my task, the presentation, the estimation, in some wise, of Weir Mitchell's generous contributions to the literature of his time. And foremost in our approach, let us note that in his admirable and simultaneous practice of two arts, Dr. Mitchell was true to an exceedingly early tradition: for was not Apollo, the god himself, alike "physic's and poesy's king"? It would be interesting to inquire what there is in the education and practice of medicine that has produced—in English letters at least—so many doctor-poets, doctor-novelists, doctor-essayists. It is easy to see why our lawyers turn for their intellectual diversions to history usually, and the dry appraisal of facts; and why some of our divines have transferred their mental activities from the abstractions of theology to the abstractions of philosophy. Is it that the physician—dare I say in this presence the physician of the school that sees in the patient a fellow man, not a mere subject for diagnosis and experiment—is closer to bare humanity after all than either the custodian of our worldly possessions or the guide to our problematic spiritual future? As far back as the very year of the birth of Shakespeare, a notable London physician, William Bullein, diversified his professional practice and publication by writing *A Dialogue against the Fever Pestilence,* which is no medical book despite the title, but a vital piece of fiction, realizing character and pondering deeply on human nature and conduct. In Queen Elizabeth's day Thomas Campion, one of the most delightful of lyric poets, signed himself proudly "Doctor of Physic," and completed the Greek ideal by gaining a high reputation as a composer of songs, the music as well as the verses. Sir Thomas Browne, the famous author of the well-known volume *Religio Medici,* practised medicine unostentatiously at Norwich, where a king sought him out and knighted him; and, to come down to our own recent day, who among you knows not our own "Autocrat of the Breakfast Table," Oliver Wendell Holmes, charming poet and trenchant epigrammatist, the scholarly literary diversions of the late Sir William Osler, and the interesting poetry of Sir Ronald Ross, discoverer of the disease-bearing mosquito, winner of the Nobel Prize, between all three of whom and Dr. Mitchell there was so agreeable an interchange of letters, as set forth recently in Mrs. Burr's admirable volume, *Weir Mitchell, His Life and Letters?*

It would be unfitting an occasion such as this to detail the particulars of the life of one so universally known as was Dr. Mitchell, especially to those who are gathered here, you who are his successors in the noble profession that he so ornamented, some of you, too, who knew him personally and loved him. But there are considerations that arise out of the contemplation of a life so active, so sure in its aims, so consistent and so ideal, that we cannot idly pass them by. Weir Mitchell was happy in his birth as the son of a distinguished physician in whose successful, versatile, and prosperous career he found before him an ever present example. As fortunate was he in his mother, who circled a household of children with that atmosphere of gentility and culture which was alike her birthright and the daily habit in which the family lived. To the advantages of birth and a cultivated home must be added those of educational opportunities well employed as they can only be employed by one in whom a mind of unusual alertness was supported by an excellent constitution. Young Mitchell grew up to be a tall, a handsome and dignified man. The mark of the aristocrat was on him and he lived up to a standard which demanded much, not only of others but likewise of himself. His career once chosen, Dr. Mitchell lived always in the light of day. There are no indirections, sinuosities, or underground passages to explain in his life. The inheritances of a sound body and a clean mind were his—and what two inheritances are more precious than these? And the consciousness of worth within him—which he was much too honest to pretend to conceal—gave him the serious dignity of bearing which was habitually his and caused him never to lose for a moment that fine sense of *noblesse oblige,* that recognition of the responsibilities of station which, however at variance it may be with some of our crude democratic practices, is really of the very essence of a noble humanity. I remember how at public functions and dinners the arrival, the presence of Dr. Mitchell was certain to key up the whole affair. Men did not like to talk banalities before him; in his presence they felt a half-conscious urge to rise to their best. Not that Dr. Mitchell's was the critical attitude towards those about him, much less the cynical, but that men felt instinctively that, like Browning's poet in "How It Strikes a Contemporary":

> He took such cognizance of things,
> If any beat a horse, you felt he saw;
> If any cursed a woman, he took note
> Yet stared at nobody—you stared at him,
> And found less to your pleasure than surprise
> He seemed to know you and expect as much.

But to the making of a character as commanding, as assured as this there must go more, in this life as it is, than an enviable stock and uniformly happy surrounding conditions. Mankind no less than the crops of the field needs the plow and the harrow; and for us to conceive of Dr. Mitchell as merely one of those fatuous monstrosities of the imagination called "Fortune's darling," is wholly to misunderstand him. There was struggle in his life, the struggle to the front and the jostling, the elbowing, and the secret thrust of envy in the process. This part of Dr. Mitchell's story belongs rather to his professional career than here; but I must remind you that whenever a man assumes leadership in this world of ours, there are likely to be captious inquiries as to "why?" though they come, for the most part, from runners far behind in the race for distinction, if not already out of it. When Dr. Mitchell's keen, practical, and foreseeing mind hit upon some notable lead in his profession, or when, as was constantly recurrent, success crowned some daring and original innovation of his in matters which it would be an impertinence in me to attempt to explain before an audience such as this—there were not wanting malignant cries of "quack" and "charlatan." To be successful and triumphant where others have failed is an offense in the eyes of mediocrity; and it is amazing to observe how apparently unconscious this well-poised man trod unerringly forward, despite insidious criticism that might have abashed a lesser man. But jealousy in his profession was soon outlived, and the approval of the discerning, which was always his, soon gave the keynote to a popularity and an acceptance that has been granted to very few men. Into the family sorrows and bereavements that were Dr. Mitchell's, it becomes us not to pry, except to remind you that *these* are the very teeth in that "harrow of God," as our forefathers used profanely to call it, that goes over the soul of man to its laceration, to its chastening and refinement and—would that we could as devoutly believe with these our forefathers—to its perfection in a better world than ours. I well remember meeting Dr. Mitchell not long after he had suffered the latest, perhaps the most complete of his bereavements, the loss of his only daughter, who was young, gifted, beautiful, with everything to have lived for. I had not seen him for some months; and I faltered such condolences as I could express, hoping that the pressure of my hand might carry something of the feeling that I had for him. His words were, "Yes, yes; but *I* still have my sons: but for her—" and he could utter neither name—"*she* was her all." The shadow had fallen, the day was no longer lit with the sun; there was a deeper discernible droop of the shoulder, less light in those kindly eyes.

It was one of the characteristics of Dr. Mitchell's fine imaginative mind that he at times built up out of the possibilities (shall we call them?) of a subject, an event, or a personality, a structure which he came generously to accept as a reality. The Civil War had broken one of his kinsmen, whose latter existence is described as "one of increasing irregularity, wandering and uncertainty." Dr. Mitchell had strained his then slender resources again and again loyally to support him and extricate him from difficulties, hopeless of any outcome or solution except that which death at last did bring. But over the mantel in that charming, that memorable room, the library of Dr. Mitchell's residence on Walnut Street, there hung the sword and belt this very kinsman had carried in the war, the dedicated memento of a hero who potentially might have died for his country, now revered for the good that once was in him, weaknesses forgiven and forgotten in his grave. Does any one of you feel disposed to mock at such a loyal reconstruction? The thing told as it ought to have been, not as it unhappily actually had fallen out? Such myths are fashioned, as was this, in the active forge of an imaginative and creative mind, by the charity and generosity of a kinsman's heart. Would that there were more such mythology, more idolatrous worship, if you like, rather than that scrutinizing malignancy, as in some of our contemporary biography, that seeks to see to it only too surely that the evil that men do shall live after them in livid perpetuity, and our little good lie deep interrèd with our bones.

But it is time that we get on to the consideration of Weir Mitchell as a writer, as one who gave the wholesome pleasure that the novel, in the hands of competence, can give, and the choicer joy to the more select few that arises out of poetry. In Dr. Mitchell's as yet unpublished autobiography, which Mrs. Burr has so judiciously employed, the author tells us of his boyhood's reading: *Robinon Crusoe, The Arabian Nights, Captain Cook's Voyages,* and a huge volume of LaVega on *The Conquest of Mexico.* "My habit," he says, "was to lie on my belly on the floor of my room and read and read. I read no poetry, but fact or fiction came all alike to me." The books in his father's library he describes as "many and good, and we were taught to use encyclopædias, to read aloud and to talk at our meals of our reading." What better foundation for the future novelist! We do not find a similar passage telling us what led this active young mind to an interest in poetry; but in the list of Dr. Mitchell's writings appended to Mrs. Burr's biography, the first item dated 1846 is a poem entitled *To a Polar Star;* and in 1846 the author was but twenty years of age. Dr. Mitchell was widely read in the English poets, not alone contemporaries and the greater names that everybody quotes glibly. I remember his once lending me offhand from his shelves a copy of *The Remains of Fulke Greville,* 1633, an out-of-the-way, difficult, and interesting poet, unknown to most of the literary pundits gathered together at the moment, but familiar enough to our host. As to his own verse, Dr. Mitchell followed the advice of Dr. Holmes that he postpone the public avowal of poetry until he reached forty years of age, and no volume of his poetry appeared until 1882, although he published anonymously from time to time. As to this form of his literary expression, Dr. Mitchell declares: "I have written verse, almost all of it since I was fifty": a somewhat remarkable declaration in view of the prevalent opinion that youth alone is the productive period among poets.

Dr. Mitchell's first essay into fiction was "The Case of George Dedlow," anonymously published in *The Atlantic Monthly* in 1866. This short story departed from the prevailing war-tale in describing not the glory of the charge or the adventures of escape, but the physical and mental sufferings and emotions of a man who had been hopelessly maimed, told, all of it, "with the veracity of a clinical report." Despite a burlesque intention that seems clear towards the end, the story was taken by its first readers so seriously that a subscription was taken up for the unlucky victim of so much mutilation and suffering. In this story, as later in "Roland Blake," "In War

Time," and in "Westways," the novelist sketched variously from the life that he had known so intimately in his incessant medical service in the Civil War; for although his posts of trust and management did not take him to the front, his experience was rich and his personal observation was ever alert to seize and fix those precious realities of life that are the subject-matter of the novelist. These are good stories and worthy of reading today. Professor Quinn, distinguished historian of our American literature, has recently remarked that "those who believe that the authors of *An Appeal to Arms* and *All Quiet on the Western Front* [have] discovered a new method of describing war, should read 'The Case of George Dedlow' "; and, further, that "long before Stephen Crane wrote *The Red Badge of Courage* [Weir Mitchell] had painted the real feeling of the soldier before the battle," and studied to the life the devious reflexes and strange contradictions of "the psychology of cowardice."

Dr. Mitchell was more than fifty years of age when he published his first novel, and it was inevitable that a writer of his gifts and his tastes should reach out beyond any one kind of story into the wider reaches of history and romance. I do not set much store on the neat little boxes of division and discrimination which historians of literature are so diligent to construct. Life would not be life, if it were not so real; as little would it be real, if it were not likewise so incurably romantic. For romance is the atmosphere of life, and nobody lives in a vacuum. Dr. Mitchell realized this to the full in his fiction, whether the emphasis was on what we now call psychology, as in Constance Trescott's determined and unavertible vengeance, or in the curious dual personality of Sibel Maywood in *Doctor North;* whether the major stress was on the romance of Philadelphia Revolutionary days as in *Hugh Wynne,* and in the fine historical portraiture of Washington, Hamilton, and Arnold in *The Red City,* or in the daring and adventures of François in the lurid times of the French Revolution. And in each and all of these competent and finished products of the novelist's art we find that adroit intermingling of a narrative well told, personages vividly presented, conversation artistically heightened, and alertness to romantic possibilities, which the authentic artist has always recognized as inherent in all true picturings of human relations.

Dr. Mitchell, whether in his fiction or in his poetry, is apt to see things in their relations as to time rather than in their relations as to space. He is *par excellence* the *raconteur,* the narrative artist, rather than the descriptive one; not in the least that I deny the latter power in him when occasion demands. And he seems to me to be peculiarly skilful in the use which he makes of that lithe and easy dialogue which is always at his command and by which he usually contrives steadily to advance his story. *Dr. North and His Friends* and *Characteristics*—both ostensibly stories—have been criticized on the score that each is overweighted with mere conversation, interesting always, brilliant often, but little, so the critics say, to the purpose of the story. Aside from the fact that there is really story a-plenty in both, is not the table-talk, it may well be asked, of gentlefolk, its instantaneous apprehension and nice discrimination, its rapier play of wit, a part of life and society—however this particular phase of a more stately time may all but have perished from the earth in this, our hasty generation? And because we happen to be obsessed at the moment with sex-hyperconsciousness in most of our novels and with a penchant for the unclean, shall we limit the novelist in his choice of a phase of human intercourse so delightful, presented with an art so completely successful? Dr. Mitchell's dialogue has the consecutiveness and the suggestiveness of intelligent and well-bred conversation, heightened, as all literary transcripts from life must be heightened, to subserve the artistic purposes of fiction. John Hay, poet and perhaps a novelist himself, in a letter to the author, aptly says of *Hugh Wynne:* "It is written with the power, charm and certainty of genius . . . and [with] the reserve of a gentleman."

The dialogue of Dr. Mitchell's novels is what it is because the author was interested throughout his life in our beautiful English speech as an instrument of expression, artistic as well as utilitarian, because, in a word, Dr. Mitchell was himself a master conversationalist. Anybody can question and answer; for mere talk even an interlocutor is unnecessary. The imparting of information to the uninformed is monologue. The miscellaneous bandying about of commonplaces is chatter. Conversation is quite another thing; for conversation demands not only brains, but an approximate mental and social equality among those who take part in it. More, conversation is less a matter of education and information than of culture and refinement of apprehension; for conversation is the flowering of gentle breeding. It has been one of the privileges of my life to have known two Philadelphia circles, or perhaps better, centers, in which the flower of conversation has flourished. One is represented in certain ambrosial evenings in companionship with that admirable man, the great Shakespearean scholar, the late Horace Howard Furness; the other, with Dr. Mitchell on those unforgettable "Saturday evenings after nine," in the library of his Walnut Street home. There it was that certain choice spirits, not too many, gathered about the hearth, and words became wingèd and thoughts luminous. There the dull man brightened and the bright man scintillated; and our gracious host kept the ball of converse ever in the air, with a hint here, a leading query there, never usurping an undue share in the talk, giving every man his chance and again and again directing a suggestion into an engaging train of ideas or crowning an argument with an epigram. Talcott Williams, ready instantaneously to argue on anything, and on either side, was very likely to be there; and Harrison Morris; and Dr. Jastrow, so learned and serious that he half resented any pleasantry, regretful of the loss of time upon it. The Doctor's two sons—the doctor, John K., affable and charming, happily described as "a sort of second host," and Langdon, successful dramatist and poet; genial Charles E. Dana, admirable Frank Gummere, Owen Wister, always reserved, already a celebrity, and many more. Fragrant smoke wreathed our heads and a little table, furnished out impeccably in the corner, pleasantly propounded the interesting query "Scotch or rye?" On leaving after such an evening we younger men would go on our way, as it were, walking on air. But alas, for the brilliant things that we had heard and the brilliant things that we were half persuaded that we had said—all had vanished and become as the evaporated beads that but anon were winking at the mazer's brim. I was inclined to a half-belief that Dr. Mitchell was not a veritable human doctor, but a species of benignant Prospero, imparting to us all, by the wave of his magic wand, powers and susceptibilities not actually our own, and delighted in having thus tuned us to a pitch beyond ourselves.

And now as to Weir Mitchell, the poet. On rereading Dr. Mitchell's poetry entire, as I have, much to my pleasure, recently, I was struck at once with his versatility, the variety of his efforts in verse, a variety and versatility which we have already found so characteristic of his fiction. For here is vigorous, picturesque narrative in dramatic form, as witness the thrilling tale of "Francis Drake" or the romance of "Philip Vernon," narrative of episode in the enticing domain of Arthurian legend that attracted Milton as it has attracted our American Robinson, and that Tennyson made his own; sonnets all too few considering their excellence, lyrics, poetry of occasion, meditation, and of nature. Dr. Mitchell's is poetry of the center, never so conservative as to fall into imitation, never radical in either the neglect of the graces of his art or in a search after the startling. With all its differences in kind, it flows majestically in the current of a great tradition, the tradition of Tennyson, the tradition of Wordsworth, of Gray further back, and Milton; in our own country this too is the tradition of the great New England poets, Bryant, Whittier, Longfellow, and Lowell; but not that of Poe, least of all that of Whitman. In this splendid central flow of English verse we have poetry conceived of and practised as a humane art, capable at once of the record of man's loftiest yearnings and ideals and of the simple handling of subjects which are near and common, if you will, until lifted by the poets' art into the category of things resplendent with significance and beauty. This is very different from the method that sets its store on originality and surprise, on the saying of something that was never before said or sung, even if banal or trivial, that delights to ruffle the skirts of Mrs. Grundy and shock the sensibilities of taste and culture. I recall a certain attitude of puzzle (shall I call it?), which was Dr. Mitchell's as to his conspicuous contemporary, Walt Whitman. The doctor was much too generous a man not to concede merit, force, originality to Whitman; but he was repelled instinctively by Whitman's coarseness of fiber, his lack of reticence and his insistence on including, in his *Leaves of Grass,* passages that could not but alienate many of more delicate sensibilities than his own. Dr. Mitchell was amused, too, at

Whitman's colossal vanity, which it is fair to state, however, was much that of a child, elemental, without guile, though not wholly without humor perhaps. There was a story going at one time that Dr. Mitchell once asked Walt, somewhat mischievously, whether he thought that his, Walt's, reputation would in the end equal that of Shakespeare. And Walt replied that he had often pondered the subject, and thought that it probably would. Perhaps the gleam was not in the inquirer's eye alone.

To return to what I have called the poetry of a great tradition, here it was that Weir Mitchell found his precedents and his examples. His devotion to nature and his loving observation of her ways of use and wont are abundantly exampled in several poems of length and dignity: "The Psalm of the Waters," which appeared in a separate volume with other poems in 1890, and, stately and beautiful, "The Comfort of the Hills," to mention here no more. And it is taking nothing from our recognition of this worth to declare our American poet a devotee to that cult of this lovely visible world in a manner true to the tradition of Wordsworth, a cult in which, it will be remembered, natural objects are not observed scientifically for themselves, nor alone for their beauty, but for the influences which they exert on the experiences of the spirit in the meditations of men. There are no finer poems among Dr. Mitchell's than the meditative ones with their seasoned, temperate, generous and understanding views of mankind in his relation to the world. Such is "The Roman Campagna," "The Magnolia Flower," the touching lines on "The Grave of Keats"; and each is what it is because it touches with fine taste and sentiment the serious things of life. This stately vein of meditative musing rose to the heights of a veritably great poem in the exquisite, the poignant "Ode to a Lycian Tomb," in which speaks the voice of an overpowering bereavement. In such as this, in the lighter but scarcely less beautiful "Ode to a Sea Gull," in the spirited stanzas (which I had the honor of having read to me by the author before its appearance in print), "On a Boy's First Reading of the Play of Henry V," and in several patriotic poems of war, Weir Mitchell challenges his right to a place of distinction in this majestic procession of the poets of this English tongue of ours who have marched down to fame on the highway of a great tradition. True is our poet, too, to other hardly lesser things: a chaste and noble diction distinguished by clarity, directness, manliness, and strength, the use, not the abuse, of language; a versification, too, is his at once lithe and musical, a guiding taste and an instinct, rare among poets, as to when to hold the hand. Aside from poems already mentioned, I like exceedingly "François Villon," "Indian Summer" in a very different mode, the charming "My Castles in Spain," and the delightfully whimsical sonnet to that wraith-name "Inogen," which occurs in the *dramatis personae* of *All's Well that Ends Well,* but not as an actual personage in the play. Dr. Mitchell's muse, for the most part, was given over to dignified and serious poetry; but he could be exceedingly happy in the lighter vein. There is an attractive and witty group of his occasional verse in his *Collected Poems,* and he ruled for many a year, following in the steps of Oliver Wendell Holmes, the laureate of his profession, happy and acclaimed on many a memorable occasion. Among his occasional verses, "A Decanter of Madeira aged 86 to George Bancroft [the historian] aged 86" is a perfect example of its kind, fanciful, witty, apt, touched with genuine sentiment. And this same noble wine of our fathers inspired yet another delicious bit of raillery in the lines entitled "Madeira."

The quoting of individual beauties in poetry is much like pointing out an exquisite flower or a delicate spray of fern as our car flashes by. But when I meet with a phrase such as this:

> The tattered livery of the ragged birch

or:

> And earthward loitering the leaves go by,

I know that I am in the presence of an observer as well as a lover of nature. And when I meet with the lines:

> Nature lays
> A woman's hand upon the troubled heart,

or:

> Ivy flung like cloaks of green
> Upon the worn and mottled wall,
> Forgotten centuries ago
> By burghers' dames at evenfall,

I know that I am in the presence of a poet as sensitive to sentiment as to beauty. Not Wordsworth himself could more adequately have stated his creed in the single line:

> There is a heritage in simple things;

and there is the essence of wisdom as of epigram in

> Today is thine—tomorrow art thou death's.

Let us return to the man; for, view human achievement as we will, the man is greater than his works; however it is they alone that remain with us, memorials of the verve, the indomitable spirit, the wisely directed activity that produced them. I like to think of Weir

Mitchell as a reincarnation of that vital, exuberant spirit of the Italian Renaissance that made the grandee a connoisseur, a patron of arts and one practised in the practicalities of rule and war as well as in the graces of gentle living; the spirit in another aspect that made Michael Angelo not only a great sculptor, a great painter, and a writer of sonnets, but an architect and a military engineer as well; the spirit that stretched the curiosity of men like Titian and Cellini to a species of universal virtuosity in a multiplicity of human activities. Dr. Mitchell loved life and he loved color. He was a gallant sight to behold in his scarlet Edinburgh gown, his noble head crowned with a soft velvet Oxford doctor's cap. And why should not a man love life and color, and not also frankly avow it? Dr. Mitchell loved praise and coveted appreciation; and again, why should he not? He had more than most men's modicum of both, and he merited it. It was Puritanism—to which I would feign prefix an adjective little suitable to the decorum of this occasion—it was Puritanism that has put us all into black and planted the dissimulation of a false modesty in our breasts. But there was more than a Renaissance spirit in Weir Mitchell; his, too, was the spirit of the humanist who seeks honestly to know that his knowledge may be useful to humanity. I mentioned Dr. Mitchell to a lady of my acquaintance the other day. "Ah!" she exclaimed, "he saved the life of my mother; I remember him, as a child; he was so grand and so kind." When I was a very young professor, a malady befell me necessitating surgeons who, in those days, came to one's house, and resulting in a leave of absence to recover in Algiers. One day a handsome coach and pair drove up to my door and Dr. Mitchell appeared, not in the least professionally, but to cheer me by his visit, and I cannot but think more particularly to reassure my anxious young wife. He asked me if I read French, to which I assented, and he sent me his own copy of a novel of George Sand, together with an even more sovereign remedy, not medical, though in a bottle. Such are the little out-of-the-way kindnesses for the doing of which most of us find little time. This busiest man of his day, having become one of the greatest physicians, extorted from life the leisure to become likewise a notable poet, a successful novelist, a faithful as well as a delightful correspondent, and an habitual doer of unconsidered kindnesses to those about him.

What did this confident, capable, and clear-visioned man think of his own literary achievements? Charged apparently with vanity by one of his correspondents, he writes frankly, as well he might: "I have something to be vain of." In the exuberance of success he declared: "I think it [*Constance Trescott*] the best American tragic novel; I could not better it." With a preference for *The Adventures of François* and a momentary avowal of *Hugh Wynne* as his highest attainment in fiction, he later recurs to the idea: "I think (under the rose) that *Constance Trescott* is the best of my books." As to his poetry, he writes respecting the "Ode to a Lycian Tomb": "Probably this is a great poem? Certainly not anywhere elsewhere in verse [of mine?] have certain emotional products of power been so reported" —and, conscious that he is practically thinking aloud as one may to an intimate friend, he adds, "ahem!" But he is not always so certain. "*Drake*," he declares in discouragement, "no one buys it, so the merit is small": an unfair enough inference assuredly as to poetry. Here it seems to me is his well-considered verdict: "About the value of certain medical gains which the world owes me I am serenely sure . . . but of the relative value of my verse I have no assurance." There is something delightfully engaging about the utterances of a man as sane and truthful as this: "My real honest pleasure," he says, "is in the work I do." And Owen Wister reports that Dr. Mitchell "never talked about the sacredness of labor, but only [of] the joy of it."

I wish there were time to tell you of his fine readings of his poetry, especially *Drake:* for his voice was sonorous, his presence impressive, his enunciation a delight; I wish there were time to tell of his clever displacing once of scarcely a dozen words in a letter of Queen Elizabeth to make it read like a bit of Shakespearean blank verse; of his interest in language which caused him to offer a prize to University students for the best essay on the Elizabethan use of "thou" and "you"; how he used to tease Horace Howard Furness with fabricated quotations from Shakespeare, but gave it up, he says, because he found that it troubled the Shakespearean. The meetings of our Franklin Inn, of which he was the honored first president, represented only one of the many functions at which he presided, always with grace and geniality. It was at one of those dinners that, leaving somewhat early, Dr. Mitchell asked me to walk up the street with him. It was a beautiful frosty night and well I remember the tall, gracious, fur-gowned figure at my side. Our discourse had been grave. We paused at last at the doorstep of his house and, turning to me, he took my hands in both of his and said: "Schelling, I am not certain that I shall see you again. I cannot hope to live much longer, but I feel that I can look back on life as worth the living and containing for me few regrets." We parted, and I never saw him again.

For summary there is no need. It is something to have known such a man and to remember that what we loved and admired in him is worthy the affection and the admiration of all good men. To have extended the reaches of scientific knowledge, to have enriched the means of curing disease and alleviating human suffering, to have given to thousands the pleasure that inheres in wholesome fiction, disturbing none, depraving no one, to have written memorable poetry to the delight of such as live in converse with the choicest of the arts, and to have attained to the full in each of these fertile fields the recognition which is so dear to our human hearts; to have served his country, his city, his profession, and his friends efficiently and faithfully; to have lived happily and blamelessly; these things are much to have been granted in this life, as they were to this incomparable man. In words once applied to William Harvey, celebrated discoverer of the circulation of the blood, and used by Dr. Mitchell in one of his happy occasional poems:

VIR DOCTISSIME
HUMANISSIME!
VALE MI' AMANTISSIME.
TUUS EX ANIMA,

thus freely paraphrased:

Doctor most erudite,
Author most humane,
Man, by all who knew him
    Best beloved,
From our hearts we salute thee!

The Study of Literature

This subject was "wished" upon me: I could never have dared a topic at once so nebulous and so bold. We are brave when we venture on a program, a prospectus or curriculum—for others. We see the landscape at large, spread as a map, and before us, its impenetrable forests pleasant mounds of green, its unfordable rivers gleaming like threads of silver in the sun, its unscalable mountains topping the scene; and we send out others to undergo the hardships of discovery and travel. Literature, scholarship, education, research: how we juggle with these fine words and flounder in the pitfalls of definition! How we employ them, words, mere words, until like the coins of commerce, smoothed, clipped, and polished, lightened in weight and their allegiance obliterated by manhandling, they cease to convey a meaning vital enough to carry an idea in the currency of life! Let us look at some of the things implied in this title and approach them warily as we might approach the difficulties of travel suggested in the figure above.

To set out on our journey, the word "literature" belongs peculiarly to the unhappy class in the coinage of our English language just alluded to, a word that by dint of constant currency and abrasion has come at last to have no particular meaning at all. When a naturalist is about to turn, let us say, to an investigation into the "Processes of Senility Among the Gastropods," he may ask his assistant to get together for him the "literature" on that very specific topic. A popular writer, preparing an article on "How Reno Became Reno," might with equal propriety seek a collection of the "literature" of divorce. On the other hand, the other day I was reading the review of a best seller—a detective story, of course; what else do we read? In this particular article the reviewer complimented the author, declaring that he, at least, was not guilty of "trying to write literature." I wonder if anybody who has consciously tried, has ever written "literature," by which, of course, we here mean a variety of writing, high in certain artistic qualities of style, happiness of expression and adequacy, sustaining a quality of thought, whatever the topic may be, that possesses—well now, just what does it possess? Notice here, my readers, that you and I are on the verge of falling into a very real danger; we are about to yield to one of the most besetting of all the many temptations of scholarship, the temptation to perpetrate a definition. In my nonage as a teacher, I once endeavored to set my intellectual house in apple-pie order. There were no kind people in those days to tell us exactly how to do this and all other things that appertain to the unhappy profession-in-leading-strings that used to be called teaching. So I formulated certain of my ideas, mixed with other people's, of course, wrapping them up in the neat little packages of definition, tied each with a string. I did even worse: I demanded of my wretched students that they memorize certain of my nice little successions of words. At one of the earliest graduates' dinners to which I had the honor of being asked, I rose on invitation to speak; the class rose, likewise, to welcome me; and, in malicious delight and with deadly precision, chanted in unison one of my favorite definitions. *That cured me:* I have not knowingly perpetrated a definition since.

To be quite serious, the perpetration of a definition is very like the making of an image of the Ever-living God. We fashion the thing with infinite pains and as infinite satisfaction; and then bow down before an idol of our own making. The rigidities of definition belong to the age of the doctrinaire, which I am trying hard to persuade myself is an age of the past, to be called by more or less meaningless and opprobrious names such, for example, as "Early Victorian." Definition hardens and codifies; definition begets sects, schools, and isms, to say nothing of controversy, uncharitableness, bigotry, excommunication, and the stake. There was once an old Greek philosopher who found the one stable quality of the universe to subsist in change, flux, an eternal state of becoming something else. Our modern Einstein, by a very different path, has arrived at much the same kind of a philosophy, knowing equally with Aristippus, that neither the things which momentarily *are,* nor their relations to other things are constant, but that life varies, waxing and waning even as we look at it, and that nothing is as it was, or will be tomorrow what it was yesterday. This is equally true, we may well believe, in the domain of thought where ideas take form momentarily in words which themselves change and vary even as we use them. Wherefore, while he must always record what he sees, what he reasons, what he infers in words as accurate as long practice can make possible, the prudent scholar is chary of conclusions and of writing Q. E. D. after demonstrations which are not, and, from their nature, cannot be, mathematical. As to your definitions, my friends, if you make them, hold them in solution, keep them fluid, ready to improve them, to adapt and adjust them, when facts, thoughts, and ideas, to you hitherto unknown or unrelated, "swim into your ken," that in such revisions and adjustments you may the more harmoniously explain the little piece of the cosmos under your contemplation and thus become broader in your vision and wiser.

But let us get back to literature; for even although we may not be so valiant as to formulate a definition, we cannot but have reasonably clear notions, at least, as to what literature is assuredly not. For example, I listened last winter to an admirable lecture by a notable professor of the Sorbonne on a pretty little romantic episode in the life of Chateaubriand when, in his youth, he was an exile in England. It was harmless and not out of character with what we already knew of the philandering disposition of that eminent Frenchman. Similarly, a few years ago, my friend Professor Harper of Princeton horrified the sedate and puritanic by setting before us, only too fully documented, a far less harmless erotic adventure of the celebrated poet Wordsworth when a youth in France, extorting from one scandalized lover of poetry at least the exclamation: "And are the critics to leave us no one celibate among the English poets!" These matters, deeply interesting as they are—dare I say, especially when they border on scandal?—are not matters literary, but biographical, and of value to a scholarly study of literature only in the proportion in which they either may or may not have affected the art of the writer. I hope that none will feel that I am laboring a trifling distinction. The study of literature is the study of an art, not a study of the artist: a distinction not unoften as important as that between the picture and the frame. It has been said of a recently very popular book about a celebrated English lyrist, by that brilliant French disciple of the late Lytton Strachey—I refer to M. Maurois—that the one thing not treated in it is Shelley's incomparable poetry. Do we want to know a poet for his poetry or for his amours? Do we want to know the conqueror of Trafalgar for his mastery of naval warfare or for his indiscretions with the fair and frail Lady Hamilton? The biography of scandal, at least, is not reasonably to be included in the category of literature, however studied or scholarly.

There are quite a number of activities about something else that are commonly mistaken, nowadays, for a study of literature. One of these is the meticulous listing of authorities which we denominate bibliography, a very necessary and proper thing in its place, but as applicable to any other subject as to literature, and by us, in this day and generation, ostentatiously overdone. Still other such activities are much of our minute identifications of the personages of fiction with actual contemporaries on the preposterous assumption that genius is essentially unimaginative; our hunting out of sources and of parallels of thought, wording, figures of speech and the like, to ascertain if perhaps somebody may not have purloined something from somebody else or whether a given author did or did not write the works commonly attributed to him. Again, there is—to emulate Polonius—the historico-allusive, the politico-allegorical or the poetico-philosophical interpretation, any one of which may be put upon some harmless old work with the intent to prove that it was written with a deep and Machiavellian purpose, mystically to convey a significance which it has been reserved to the superior intelligence of the scholarship of the twentieth century to fathom and expose. The metropolis of scholarship is a very large town, and there are byways and alleys in it as well as magnificent and forthright streets and boulevards. There, too, are purlieus and outlying districts, of the relation of which to the authentic inhabitants of the great city we may be somewhat doubtful; and besides, there are haunts in which things flourish, in common with human nature elsewhere, the investigation of which is really little to the purpose in hand. To leave our figure, neither history nor biography, neither bibliography nor philosophy, nor grammar, nor prosody, nor textual criticism, philosophy, nor æsthetics constitutes, each in itself, the study of literature, howsoever each and all are ancillary and often indispensable. For when all is said, the heart and soul of what we are seeking in the scholarly study of any literary product is a closer touch with, and a truer understanding of, that work for what it *is,* alike as the production of a certain man and as the outcome of the contemporary and other conditions which made that man the man he was. The question as to whether the man transcends his work or the work the man is not quite so idle as the query whether the egg precedes the chicken or the chicken the egg. What we can learn concerning the life of any man of genius rarely distinguishes him conspicuously above others similarly circumstanced in life. He lived and loved and sinned as the average man has lived and loved and sinned. It is that in which the subject of our inquiry rose above his fellows, that which made him the man he became—it is that that we want to know of him: his deeds, if a man of action; his public achievements, if a figure in history; the products of his art, if painter or poet. Unless a man's achievements transcend his personality, he is scarcely more than a subject for social or anthropological scrutiny so far as any scholarly interest in him is concerned.

Leaving these activities in something else for what each of them may be worth, our contemporary study of literature is characterized by a number of quite definite features. First of all, we are exceedingly *skeptical* and accept nothing—sometimes not even the multiplication table. This in itself is an excellent quality when not referable to some defect in education or to that modern arrogance of spirit that habitually ignores the past or patronizes and belittles it. There is actually nothing whatever especially to recommend the present moment except the purely accidental circumstance that it *is* the present moment. Again we are amazingly *liberal,* and frequently and at the same time, *narrow* to a degree. This is not a paradox; for our willingness to let everybody think as he may and pursue his way as he will is born, only too often, of a small-spirited indifference as to anything in which we may not happen ourselves to be momentarily interested, and results, like our skepticism, from the limited range of our education. To the scandal of some, be it remarked in passing that no one thing so tends to *deliberalize* scholarship as the educational perversity which leads us so persistently to throw the weight of our preferences as to courses in college and school on concrete, utilitarian, and quasi-vocational subjects. Scholarship, conceived of as no more than a process devoted to the accumulation of information, must always face the limitations of narrowness and a cheap and hand-to-mouth utilitarianism; for no man can know it all, and no topic can be justly apprehended, except in its relations to that general body of knowledge in which subsists the culture of the world. Scholarship, like life itself indeed, is only too often conceived of as a game in which the one great mandate is "keep your eye on the ball," and contrive, however you do it, to "get by," this last a trick most frequently turned less by skill and knowledge than by taking advantage of the ignorance or inadvertence of your adversary. Scholarship is more, let us hope, than a game of chance, or even wholly of skill. Veritable scholarship is the flower of a wide knowledge, reading, and acquaintance with things as they are and as they have been interpreted by the wise who have preceded us; and I read with a blush the English review of an American book in which attention is slyly called to the mangling of a Latin quotation or the misspelling of a classical name. It will not have escaped some that a chief reason for this narrowness of spirit, which is not to be denied as a characteristic of much of our contemporary scholarly activity, lies in the circumstance that most of us are possessed of too merely the specialist's training, or, to put it in another way, we have been trained too early and too wholly in our specific vocation or profession to the loss and detriment of that more general knowledge and culture which should form the foundation of all specialization. You can get more about chemistry or botany or physics into a youngster whom you have preordained shall be a doctor, if you begin these subjects, carefully specialized for medical purposes, in his freshman year, or even in the preparatory school. But you will pay a price for it; and that price will involve the loss of much not to be recovered by any means in later professionally absorbed and less impressionable years. You have lost in the man; and have you really gained in the doctor? I rejoice in a frequent repetition of the paradox: "The best specialist is the man who knows the most about other things."

Now it is precisely this condition of blindness as to anything outside of your particular "game of ball" or mine, that causes us at times so seriously to suffer in our scholarship from an absence of that large spirit of *disinterestedness* which it has always seemed to me is so essential in any pursuit of the truth. And by this spirit of disinterestedness I mean the pursuit of scholarship for what there is in the activity itself and its outcome, and a reasonable freedom in this from ulterior designs and purposes that make for publicity and personal advancement. Knowing this spirit little in our education, we cannot carry it over into our later scholarly pursuits. I once knew a notable professor who deliberately and successfully worked up quite a reputation. He did not write books, nor often even considerable articles, but addicted himself to the incessant publication, anywhere, everywhere, of notes, emendations, comments, queries—each and all of them carefully signed. He rarely read anything without raising some question about it, and always in print; and he was expert in the thrust and parry of controversy. Indeed, he used cynically to remark that a note of ten lines or the emendation of a single word bulked as large in a man's bibliography as the title of a work in three volumes. Now, no one can deny that this man was *interested* in scholarship, such as his was; he was not *disinterested*. He was seeking not the truth, but, shall we say, the bubble reputation at a risk more safe than at the cannon's mouth?

But there are other characteristics of our contemporary scholarship. Considering that we find ourselves, in the academic study of literature in America at least, in a fourth or at best in a third generation, ours is less a harvest than a garnering of what remains. Hence, like Autolycus, we are constrained to become "great snappers up of unconsidered trifles," and our search for the bagatelles of literature is endless. To illustrate from my own shop, I remember an article in which the writer endeavored to prove that Hamlet's fine allusion to "this most excellent canopy"—and the poet immediately adds "the air, look you, this brave o'er hanging firmament, this majestical roof fretted with golden fire"—is not to be regarded an allusion to the glorious luminaries of heaven, but to the fretting of golden stars which the learned have discovered adorned a species of sound-board known as "the heavens" that hung over the stage of the Elizabethan playhouse. This is at least ingenious: as ingenious as it is absurd. The curious might collect libraries of like absurdities. In the purview of this kind of scholarship, trifles become mountains and mountains dwindle into molehills. For scholars such as these are visited alike by the wraiths of doubt and the hallucinations of certainty: doubts as to whether any simple and logical interpretation of anything in the past can possibly be the right one, "certainties" that our own complicated surmises are more likely to arrive at truth than the plain evidences of those who were conversant contemporaneously with the matters in question. We labor under the delusion that all matters historical and literary are capable of as definite a solution as an equation in algebra. We suffer from a strange infatuation that our own cleverness is certain to succeed where others—with their inferior "intelligence quotients"—have failed. And we are possessed by a stubborn unwillingness to confess that the evidence is insufficient or at the least inconclusive. We hate to class with Socrates, who knew at least that he did not know and did not hesitate to acknowledge his ignorance.

There has never been an age in which the literary and artistic productions of the past have been so scrutinized and exploited as in this of ours. We edit everything and everybody; we rewrite, revise, review, and rearrange; ours is the heydey of criticism, of commentary, of controversy and correction. Economic conditions alone appear somewhat to limit our printing of everything, and it would be a nice question to determine: "Do we read anything approaching as much as we write?" Not content with mature and professional activity, we employ the study of literature, properly enough I am sure, as a means of education; but, here again, we seem only too commonly less intent on what the student reads than that we shall keep him eternally writing. I am no pedagogue. I even dislike the assumptions implicit in the much-abused title "Professor," but it is impossible that some of the dust of the schoolroom should not have adhered to an old teacher. Here are some of its particles. I believe in the writing of themes for students of all degrees and I believe in the study of literature, not by talking about movements and tendencies and periods of transition, but by a close reading and study of the literary productions that we want to know. As to the art of "how to write," I have a conviction that it is better to write about something with which the writer possesses some acquaintance than to cram up on topics little known, and by this run the risk of merely repeating what has been recently read. I believe that it is better to cultivate and draw out what there may be in a student rather than to attempt to train him after Stevenson's famous theory of "the sedulous ape," to write somewhat—oh, how somewhat!—after the manner of somebody else. And I am convinced that all a student's writing, from the preparatory school—if they still teach so simple a process as writing there—to the graduate thesis itself, is a process in the nature of an exercise and not to be thought of for a moment as concerned with the production of a really finished product. Least of all do I feel that we should sink our voices in a hushed and reverent awe at a mention of that blessed word "research," and feel that our young Ph.D.'s are a splendid phalanx of indefatigable warriors, beating back the realms of darkness and ignorance with the overpowering brilliancy of their discoveries. On the basis of these beliefs, I regard the enforced publicity of the published thesis as one of the absurdities of our American educational customs; although I should be willing to grant the right to print an occasional thesis as the concession of a very high honor in the case of a very unusual merit. I grant that it is not irrational to teach the student how to get together a book, if it shall happen at some time or other that he may have occasion to write one. But to insist upon this laborious exercise, carried out to the correction of the last comma, for every young man and woman who seeks to please his vanity or better his financial status as a teacher by the acquisition of a degree—all of this seems to me the height of absurdity.

Lastly of the features of our contemporary study of literature, there is the stress we lay upon *method:* indeed, there is no one thing in which we pride ourselves more highly. However weak the thought or trivial the subject-matter, the strength of Hercules or Samson is in the handling and presentation; from the little bow of acknowledgment in the prefatory note "to the great men and the great libraries that have helped me," to the embroidery of footnotes, the beautifully alphabetical bibliography, the learned appendices, which catch and hold the superfluities of the subject, and the laborious index—*all* is as it should be. And it is printed, often on fine paper, sometimes to the temporary financial embarrassment of the unhappy author—for he has to pay for it in more ways than one—published with a pretty little flourish and then, unwept, unsung, unread, and perhaps even unreviewed, is happily forgotten. Let me say as to method: There are eighty-seven different ways in which to order and arrange adequately the subject-matter for a good thesis. To the next worker under my guidance, I shall say: "It is your business to discover an eighty-eighth."

With our emphasis on method and novelty—"a contribution to the sum total of human knowledge," unctuous commencement orators call it—and with our further innate love of the concrete, of facts that you can get your feet on, there are serious limitations on the American graduate thesis in literary subjects. On this topic I would seriously submit that, granted that the thesis is an exercise and at best journey-work, it is the process, and evidence of the student's competence in that process, that we are after, rather than any demand that the product shall display the overprized quality of novelty and actually discover something new. The problems of Euclid are new to him who approaches them for the first time, and the processes of scholarship are often cultivated as well on a known problem as on one which has only novelty to recommend it. There is of course an obvious enough reason for our preference of a fact to a truth. Mere diligence may stumble over a new fact. There are closets and garrets still to ransack and there always will be. It is not so easy to reason justly upon the basis of things as they are and transmute them into that higher order that obtains among the categories of truth. It is something to write a good book on any topic, and it seems a pity that our system of education must make so many of us accessories at least to the writing of so many bad ones. There are printed theses extant on the title-pages of which the name of a long-suffering and self-abnegating teacher, the aider, initiator and abettor of it all, should stand at least with that of the avowed author. So to place the teacher's name, however, might be little to his credit and less to that of the budding Ph.D., thus nudged and buffeted into a degree. There are theses in which we who are teachers have had our reluctant part, that we blush to remember. But let me hasten to add that there are others—nor are they few, our compensations for much else—which we are proud to have stimulated, work genuinely and independently done, a credit to the writers and an assurance as to the future. I for one find no deterioration in the intelligence of the rising generation, nor in their ability and power to carry on. Their shortcomings are only too heavily chargeable to us who have sought at times unwisely to lead them. Perhaps there is no wiser dispensation of Providence than that which has provided the young with an efficient protective armor—by no means always that of stupidity—against some of the processes of the education that we seek to inflict upon them.

There is one other topic as to this matter of the study of literature on which I should like to touch, and that is the question of subsidy and direction. I have just mentioned the student who needs merely a hint, a suggestion; out of his independent, his individual kind, veritable scholars are made. By implication at least there is his more numerous fellow, who needs his subject chosen for him, his plan made out for him, his attempts to follow it corrected, changed, adjusted, tempered—"God tempers the wind to the shorn lamb"—who, in short, needs everything. And we his teachers, miserable sinners that we are, crutch and sustain his feeble efforts and, what is more, are confidently expected to do this sort of thing. Our modern education supplies everything—except brains. But it is less of this pampering than of subsidy and direction that I speak here. In the old days —and we old fellows always remember the old days with the halo of a romantic sanctity about them—well, in the old days, ours were all the rigors of the game. It was your own affair if you wanted to become a scholar, and you might starve if you liked for it. I know a man who was twenty years writing a book on a topic of his own choosing. He journeyed, during that interval, some six or seven times abroad, where the books then were. And it never occurred to him not to pay his own way out of his own slender teacher's pittance. Nowadays there are scholarships, fellowships, institutes and foundations and no one need work unsubsidized. You can even choose from among them which will pay you the best; and there is money to be had, almost for the asking, for books and photostats, sent to your desk, for clerical assistance, manuscripts examined and what not. There are committees to further and stimulate research, that will point out to you fertile fields and likely leads, and offer coöperation and even publication. A paternal foundation is even now furnishing "librarians of research" to stimulate not only students but backward members of faculties to greater activities in scholarship, that the pendulum may continue even more merrily to swing from time stolen from scholarship for the classroom to time stolen from the classroom for research. When I was a boy at the University of Pennsylvania, I was subjected to protectionist ideals in the study of political economy. The professor of that subject was so incessantly eloquent a protectionist that I became, and have remained, a notable exception among inhabitants of the state of Pennsylvania, a confirmed and unrepentant free-trader. I am a confirmed and unrepentant free-trader in scholarship, and seriously question the efficacy of all tariffs of direction and subsidy. The sons of Eli are educated in palaces. Are all the sons of Eli to live forever after like princes? The protégés of Rhodes are maintained at Oxford with allowances that the average of them will scarcely earn for years after they take up what are likely to be their vocations in life. Indeed, we often spend in the aggregate a sum for the exploitation of some trifle of research which might well maintain a couple of students in their endeavors to obtain an ordinary education. And it is to be remembered that the maintenance of the apparatus is coming increasingly to be far more costly than a sanguine estimate of the preciousness of the results. It is decidedly questionable if subsidy has not measurably deprived us in scholarship of much of that initiative, that independence, the vigor that is born of struggle and that is inherent in the individual, not to be extraneously directed, least of all to be strengthened by studied and ordered coöperation. You cannot keep a scholar from his book. Nor can we ever hope to make a scholar by subsidy and direction.

In these last paragraphs I fear that I have fallen somewhat into pedagogics, the cocksure science of exactly how to do it. Returning to higher ground and I trust a wider view, I still do not think that we have reason to feel discouraged as to the scholarly study of literature in this our time. We have done much in the unearthing of new material and in the ordering of the old; we have dug deep and journeyed far. It has been said that history must be rewritten in adaptation to the needs of each new generation, and this is equally true of our criticism of the thought, the art, the achievements, and the ideals of those who have gone before us. It is not that the race is as a race much wiser or that our scholars and critics in natural endowment overtop their predecessors on the highways of learning. It is rather that scholarship is now more generally diffused; there are more of us engaged in intellectual pursuits of this kind, and our attitude is more professional and, I should like to believe, our researches are more thorough and likely to stand the test of time for that reason. We are getting well away, in the study of literature at least, from the ancient dogma that the last word can be said on any topic, that anything human can be definitively done. We recognize the necessarily provisional quality of most of our judgments and, while willing to die serving our own guns, respect the soldier who mans the guns of opposite opinion. Perhaps I have been betrayed into the hyperbole of hope in this last sentence: indeed I rather fear it, when I recall that recently in a controversy involving nothing more of moment than who wrote what particular lines in what particular play, some of the best among us still confound the man with the heretical opinions he holds and thrust both out of the haven of scholarship.

"The haven of scholarship!" Accidental but happy phrase! In the turmoil and rush of this our too, too rapid modern life, with everything at flux in a state as variable and hectic as the stock market, it is good to know that there is a haven, perhaps less of rest than of a placid and ordered activity, which exists on a basis other than that of supply and demand and which is occupied with ideas and ideals untranslatable into the terms of barter and trade. Let us not forget that it is the things of the mind alone which live and propagate to the veritable progress of mankind. It is hard to kill the best that is in us, and that best is the creative power of human thought, the power that has produced our arts, our literatures, our laws, our religion, our civilization itself. In the humble and scholarly study of such assuredly lies the finest, the most disinterested, the noblest of intellectual pursuits.

Walls of Brass
A Fancy and a Parallel

When London was new to the young Shakespeare, two plays of devil-lore and magic, *Doctor Faustus* and *Friar Bacon and Friar Bungay,* were holding the public stage; one the work of the notorious Christopher Marlowe, the other that of a popular writer of fiction, Robert Greene, now chiefly remembered for his personal grudge against Shakespeare. Both plays were based on old-world stories, even then as familiar almost as the folklore of the countryside; and one of them, the story of Faustus, was destined to inspire the best poetic and musical genius of at least two modern nations. The German *Faustbuch,* whatever the intermediate channel, was the source and inspiration of Marlowe's *Tragical History of Doctor Faustus,* precisely as an old English chapbook, *The History of Friar Bacon and Friar Bungay,* was the original of Robert Greene's comedy of that title. These plays as we read them seem animated with a spirit of rivalry, the one with the other, the "white magic" of Greene's play, as the benevolent traffic with the supernatural was called, answering the malevolent or "black magic" of *Faustus.* Both have this in common, that each concerns the life, the art, and the fate of one whose ambition it was to transcend and dominate his fellow men in the brief world in which he lived, and that this ambition led him in each case to pawn his soul to the Prince of Evil thereby to attain that unhallowed end.

There is no need to repeat the familiar story of Doctor Faustus, "his damnable and deserved death," as the title of the old English

Faust Book has it, his conjuring of the devil, his deadly compact sealed with blood, his throes and agonies, as the spirits of good and evil wrestle in his heart for the possession of his soul. This is not the master work of cosmopolitan Goethe who raised the old legend of medieval devilry to a fourth dimension of modern speculative philosophy and, after bringing the gins and snares of the cleverest of devils to an overthrow of the virtue of one poor little Nuremberg maiden, transcends time, fate, and eternity in his stupendous second part to the outfacing of God as well as to the outwitting of the devil. More real, more pathetic, dare we say more dramatically effective, is Marlowe's broken torso of a complete statue with its cheap medieval *diablerie* and its simple, poignant scenes of the agony of an average human soul in straits to pay the penalty of his own sin and folly.

Faustus has pledged his soul, and to what end? that he may play petty schoolboy tricks: box the ears of England's enemy, the Pope, in "his Holiness' privy chamber" and outwit a jockey in the sale of a horse. To such ashes turn the fruits of Sodom on the lips of the sinner, whether of today or of yesterday. Verily, the old tragedy belonged to an age of greater faith than ours, an age—can we call it such?—of deeper superstition. There is a curious old anecdote extant of a contemporary performance of *Faustus,* in the provinces somewhere, apparently, and with the limited scratch company of actors that traipsed out of London in time of plague and "carried their fardels a pick-a-back," as the old phrase goes. They had reached the scene in which the Seven Deadly Sins file by in order before Faustus and Mephistopheles, each discoursing on the quality of his peculiar wickedness; and the stage direction—not designated in the old quartos—called for a dance of these deadly visitants. As they were whirling about beyond the magic circle which Faustus had drawn about him with his sword for his protection, he and his fellow actor of Mephistopheles looked upon the scene, and behold, there were, not seven devils, but eight! Now, the company was all accounted for; for the actors were few in number and the parts were doubled and doled out even threefold. So the actors of Faustus and Mephistopheles as well—the latter sadly forgetting his part—fell on their knees and cried upon God to forgive them their sins, for there was a real devil among them, while players and auditors stampeded in terror from the stricken place. The thing is ludicrous, but it represents an honest faith in the everpresence of evil among us, the deterrent, we may well believe, of many a robust sinner, a deterrent sadly to seek in this our rational and unbelieving age.

The History of Friar Bacon and Friar Bungay, the contrasted play, is less popularly known. It has been a moot question, even among scholars, as to whether there was ever a Johann Faust; or, if there was, whether he was in any wise the tamperer with forbidden studies that the figure of the dramatic Faustus represents. No such doubt hangs about Friar Bacon, who is referable to no less a person than Roger Bacon, the famous scholar of thirteenth-century Oxford. Bacon, it will be remembered, was a man of substance and station in his time, however his family had become impoverished in the feudal wars of King Henry III. Bacon gave away such wealth as he had, devoted his life to scientific study and investigation: this in an age when the theology of scholasticism had engulfed nearly all learning in its thirsty and barren quicksands. Seeking peace in the Franciscan brotherhood in despair of his long struggle to acquire learning, Bacon was forbidden to write on pain of forfeiture and penance; and only the intervention of the Pope made possible the publication of the admirable *Opus Majus* and its successors in which we find Roger Bacon anticipating his namesake Francis by some three hundred years in a daring attempt to reform the crude philosophizing processes of his time, in order to open up new sources of knowledge and to point forward the way to the enfranchisement of learning. In the comprehensive review which Roger Bacon gave the sciences of his day, grammar, philology, textual criticism, music, mathematics, nothing is forgotten; and he passes on to treat of geography, chronology, hydropathy, astrology, and optics (this last his special study), with a suggestion of improvement for each and a recognition for all in his comprehensive scheme. It is not to be wondered that, in an ignorant age, a haze of popular myth should soon have gathered about so remarkable a genius. Later times assigned to Bacon the discovery of gunpowder, the invention of the telescope and the crystal glass wherein the doings of persons at a distance were clearly reflected, the *camera obscura,* in other words; and other inventions were said to be his. As to his own age, tradition made him a conjuror whose dealings were with the powers of evil, whereby he made many "wonderful inventions of art." Among them were "instruments of navigation without a man to rowe in them, and they sayle," says the narrative of these wonders, "far more swiftly than if they were full of men"; also chariots that shall move with an unspeakable force without any living creature to steer them; flying engines; and an instrument of three fingers high "by which a man may rid himself and others of imprisonment, and whereby a man may virtually draw unto him a thousand men, will they nill they." But the greatest of Bacon's ingenuities, according to popular tradition, was the creation of a brazen head which, the incantations complete, was to have had the power of speech. To the consummation of this great work Bacon and his assistant adept in magic, Friar Bungay, labored long; and, at last, by the conjuration of the devil and their compelling power upon him, their task was finished, but for the crowning achievement, the utterance of human speech. It was then that their familiar spirit reluctantly warned them that "with the continual fume of the six hottest simples [the brazen head] should have motion and in one month's space speak; the time of the month or the day he knew not; also he told them that if they heard it not before it had done speaking all their labor should be lost."

Now Faustus, "glutted with conceit" (that is, busied with the imaginative construction of air castles), and in the ecstasy of his dreams of power, demanded of his familiar, supernatural attendant many selfish things: "gold fetched from the Indies," "orient pearl," "pleasant fruits and princely delicates"; for his was the ambition of the superman for world power, a world-wide commerce such as England fought Spain on the seas to achieve, to bring him the products of strange lands to the end that he might have dominion and the means of luxurious living. There was, however, among his behests to his familiar, one, which if not less selfish, was at least less apparently personal and that was this desire:

> I'll have them wall all Germany with brass.

So, too, Friar Bacon's avowed purpose in the contriving of the brazen head was

> By the help of devils and ghastly fiends,
> . . . ere many years or days be past,
> To compass England with a wall of brass.

The assumption of superiority to one's fellow man involves inevitably a barrier against his resentment of that assumption. And in conceiving of that barrier as compacted of metal and of that metal as brass, our ancient story-tellers may be said verily to have builded better than they knew. Of the ambitious project of Faustus to "wall all Germany with brass," we hear no more in the old story. The project fell through before more immediate and trivial things; having been once foretold, it was left to the accidents of Fate; and in the throes and agonies of his damnation Faustus soon had more personal things to think about. Unhappily, too, for the English project of Friar Bacon and Friar Bungay, the two friars at last, worn out with constant watching for the promised moment when the miraculous brazen head was at last to speak, entrusted their weighty charge to a foolish servant named Miles. Miles was to watch while they slept and wake them at the supreme moment. Let the old book continue the story:

[Now] after some noyse the head spake these two words, TIME IS. Miles, hearing it speak no more, thought his master would be angry if he waked him for that, and therefore he let them both sleepe, and began to mock the head in this manner: "Thou brazen-faced head, hath my master tooke all these paines about thee, and now doest thou requite him with two words, TIME IS? . . . If thou canst speak no wiser, thou shalt sleepe till doomes day for me: TIME IS!" . . . After half an houre had passed, the head did speake againe, two words, which were these, TIME WAS. Miles respected these words as little as he did the former, and would not wake them, but still scoffed at the brazen head, that it had learned no better words, and have such a tutor as his master. . . . Thus Miles talked and sang till another half-houre was gone: then the brazen head spake again these words, TIME IS PAST; and therewith fell down, and presently followed a terrible noyse, with strange flashes of fire, so that Miles was halfe dead with feare. At this noyse the two Fryers awaked, and wondred to see the whole roome so full of smoake;

but that being vanished, they might perceive the brazen head broken and lying on the ground. . . . "Out on thee, villaine!" said Fryer Bacon; "thou hast undone us both: hadst thou but called us when it did speake, all England had been walled round with brasse, to its glory and our eternal fames!"

In these two old tales, as the dramatists treated them, there are several passages remarkably pertinent, if not prophetic, of the straits in which the world lay struggling yesterday, the net in which it lies entangled even today. What a superlative superman is Faustus, and how admirably he voices the abiding Teutonic ambition for world dictatorship and empire!

> O, what a world of profit and delight
> Of power, of honor, of omnipotence
> Is promised to the studious artizan!

("Studious artizan" is good Elizabethan for subtly plotting diplomatist.) He thus continues:

> All things that move between the quiet poles
> Shall be at my command: emperors and kings
> Are but obeyèd in their several provinces,
> Nor can they raise the wind, nor rend the clouds;
> But his dominion that exceeds in this,
> Stretcheth as far as doth the mind of man.

Again:

> Shall I make spirits fetch me what I please,
> Resolve me of all ambiguities,
> Perform what desperate enterprise I will?

. . . . . .

I'll have them read me strange philosophy.

(Could the Nietzschean philosophy be better designated with its novel ethical code?)

And tell the secrets of all foreign kings.

(The admirable German system of espionage in foreign countries has been unequaled in the history of the world.)

I'll have them wall all Germany with brass.

(It may be doubted if a nation has ever been better prepared than was Germany for the Great War, and now for the next.)

I'll levy soldiers with the coin they bring
And men in armor shall appear.

(Germany's military system is based on wide commerce and subtle finance.)

And reign sole king in all our provinces.

(Prussian political preëminence.)

Yea stranger engines for the brunt of war,
Than was the fiery keel of Antwerp's bridge,
I'll make my servile ministers invent.

(The supremacy of the Krupp gun, possibly also poison gas, is foretold.)

I'll be great emperor of the world
And make a bridge thorough the moving air
To pass the ocean with a band of men.

(Even the Zeppelin invasion of England is here foretold and in what follows the ever present help of the Almighty.)

Having thee [the God of the superman] ever to attend on me,
To give me whatsoever I shall ask,
To tell me whatsoever I demand,
To slay my enemies and aid my friends,
And always be obedient to my will.

Friar Bacon was less the superman. In the play, it is true, he is victorious in a match at magic with one Vandermast, a rival in his art. Vandermast conjures Hercules to appear in person before the assembled court; but Friar Bacon constrains Hercules by his superior power to carry Vandermast home on his back to Vandermast's native Germany. My powers of vaticination do not enable me to figure forth precisely the meaning of this. Perhaps it has to do with commercial jealousy, or English objection to the notorious pre-war German industrial invasion of England. But in the days when he, too, was "possessed," Bacon leaves us in no doubt of the precise nature of his political ambition:

I have contrived and framed a head of brass

. . . . . .

And I will strengthen England with my skill,
That if ten Caesars,

(here read most prophetically Mussolinis),

lived and reigned in Rome
With all the legions Europe doth contain,
They should not touch a grass of English ground.

It is notable that Friar Bacon is a humane magician, practising "white magic" for the welfare of mankind—a clear allusion to the long-praised white man's burden; and when, at last, his meddling with forbidden things causes evil and his "glass prospective worketh many woes," the Friar abjures his art and "pyromantic spells," as England has cleverly abjured her empire of conquest and dominion, making it over into a sisterhood of nations, and thus acquiring, like the good Friar, a reputation for benevolence, besides cannily cheating the devil.

Let us leave these old wives' tales and curious parallels of a forgotten lore. The modern dictator, tyrant, superman is a disappointment as we compare him with Faustus and Friar Bacon. The German Faustus, after all, sought metaphysical knowledge as well as worldly power: a combination at one time characteristic but now no longer true of German *Kultur;* and the English Friar had a benevolent quirk in his aspirations, however such benevolence is wont to thrust itself upon the object, whether he yearns to become civilized or Christianized and protected with walls of brass or not. Other earlier supermen were characterized in their ideas and their actions by a species of natural brute candor: Machiavelli in his frank theories anticipating Treitzschke, as the Alexanders, Caesars, and the Napoleons, magnificent ravening beasts that they were, anticipated in their activities the modern manipulators of Big Berthas, underseas-crafts, Zeppelins dropping murder, and masters in the art of chemistry diffusing poison gas and breeding the microbes of pestilence. More, these devotees of might as the god over right were honestly consistent, treading with ruthless heel on guilt and innocence alike. Never did one of them look backward or downward at the bleeding forms that their victorious tread had marred from the likeness of men; their pitiless eyes were ever forward for new foes or upward in adoration of the terrible god of carnage whom they had invoked, whether his name was Moloch, Ares, Mars, or Thor. Our modern overlords are weak in the knees, unstable of faith in their own gods, explanatory in printed books and documented excuses, concerned about the opinion of the brute multitude that happens as yet to be out of the reach of their guns. Life to these godlets and godlings is a dirty game, each gamester outwitting his fellow in chicanery and by violence at need. As cruel as was ever Attila, if substituting the ruin by persecution and confiscation for honest pillage and slaughter, their cunning is that of the rat, with their eternal marchings *en masse,* their ordered salutes, plebiscites, and jubilations, overwhelming, as do the rodents, by weight of numbers. Marlowe's Faustus, having had his will, took his medicine of damnation like a man; Goethe's Faust contrived by the sinuosities of German metaphysics and the admirable quality of his *Weltkultur* to have both his will in this world and his salvation in the next. Can it be that our modern evangelists of a higher civilization at the cannon's mouth are not really supermen at all, but only of paltry stature, masquerading in the stolen regalia of the Caesars and the pomp of the heroes of the Walhalla of Wagnerian opera?